Current Events

Contemporary Issues for Classroom Debates, Discussions, and Writing

Written by Diane Sylvester
Illustrated by Bev Armstrong

2003 · The Learning Works

The Learning Works

Illustrator: Bev Armstrong
Book design: Studio E Books, Santa Barbara, Calif.
Cover illustrator: Rick Grayson
Cover designer: Barbara Peterson
Project director: Linda Schwartz

Toto

Contents

Educational Topics

Medical & Scientific Topics

Governmental Topics

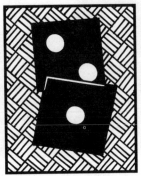

To the Teacher

Current Events is a book of controversial, contemporary issues relevant to students and society. The topics are of local, national, and international importance, and are written for students in grades 5 through 8. The purpose of the book is to encourage research, decision making, and knowledgeable discussions and debates on topics that puzzle even the great thinkers, politicians, and educators of the world.

Many students are confused and perplexed by controversy and have difficulty making decisions or stating opinions. *Current Events* requires students to question their beliefs and attitudes and encourages them to compare and contrast viewpoints. These skills are the foundation of the discipline of philosophy. It is important to know what you stand for and why.

The topics presented cover many school disciplines, including science, politics, economics, health and medicine, language arts, and social studies. Each topic includes:

Background information (What's the Issue?)
Arguments on both sides of the issue (Focus on the Controversy)
Activities and projects (Activities)
Supplemental activities appropriate for gifted students (Extended Activities)

The activities and projects following each topic are based on current academic content standards. They are written to promote development and use of higher-level thinking skills as outlined in Bloom's Taxonomy, and provide opportunities for discussion and debate among students. Students are encouraged to use a variety of methods to communicate information, including factual and creative writing, oral presentations, audio-visual presentations, art, drama, and charts and graphs.

Although the information presented for each topic is as current as possible, topics involving science, medicine, cultural mores, and judicial decisions may change over time.

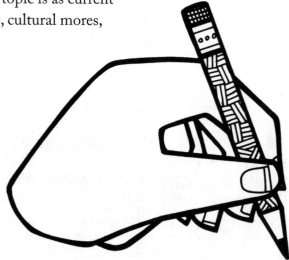

4

OVERVIEW OF THE HIGHER LEVELS OF BLOOM'S TAXONOMY

Application: apply, choose, demonstrate, dramatize, employ, illustrate, interpret, operate, practice, schedule, sketch, solve, use, write

Analysis: analyze, appraise, calculate, categorize, compare, contrast, criticize, differentiate, discriminate, distinguish, examine, experiment, question, test

Synthesis: arrange, assemble, collect, compose, construct, create, design, develop, formulate, manage, organize, plan, prepare, propose, set up, write

Evaluation: appraise, argue, assess, attach, choose, compare, defend, estimate, judge, predict, rate, core, select, support, value, evaluate

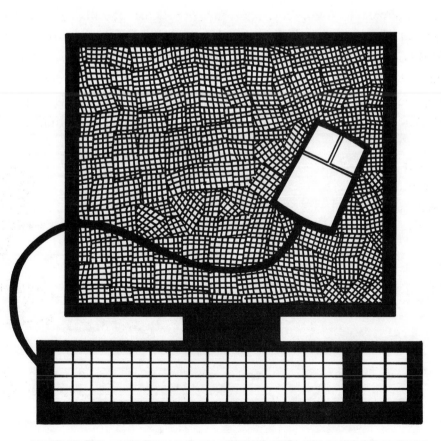

Overview of Some Academic Content Standards Presented in Current Events

Science
Understands ethics associated with scientific study

Understands that many scientific innovators had difficulty breaking through accepted ideas of their time

Knows ways in which science and society influence one another

Knows ways in which technology has influenced the course of history

Knows ways in which technology and society influence one another

Language Arts
Writes expository compositions

Writes persuasive compositions

Gathers and uses information for research purposes

Uses a variety of resource materials to gather information for research topics

Participates in group discussions

Social Studies
Identifies major discoveries in science and technology and describes their social and economic effects on the physical and human environment

Gives examples of the causes and consequences of current global issues, such as the consumption of natural resources and the extinction of species, and suggests possible responses by various individuals, groups, and nations

Explains how and why events may be interpreted differently depending upon the perspectives of participants, witnesses, reporters, and historians

Explains the need for laws and policies to regulate science and technology

Explains how laws are developed, how the purposes of government are established, and how the powers of government are acquired, maintained, justified, and sometimes abused

Locates, organizes, and uses relevant information to understand an issue of public concern, take a position, and advocate the position in a debate

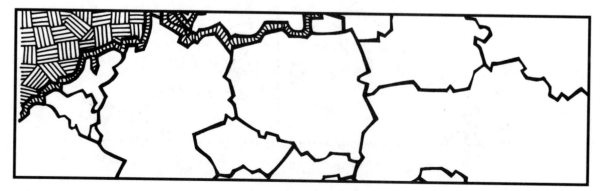

6

Discussions and Debates

The English word *democracy* comes from the Greek word *demokratia*, meaning "rule by the people." Democracy first flourished in ancient Athens after the statesman Cleisthenes (late sixth century B.C.) initiated a series of major reforms. For example, any man with full citizenship could go to the assembly, where he could speak and vote freely. Citizens met regularly in public assemblies to vote on state policies. Their voting was preceded by debate, and it was the public debates that helped decide how the city was run.

Today, debate is still essential to democracy, even though the democratic process has changed from the times of Cleisthenes. Debates occur every day on the floor of the United States Senate and House of Representatives. They occur at the United Nations, in businesses and schools, and probably in private homes. Some debates are carried on in newspapers and magazines (in editorials and letters to the editor), and on radio or television. Debates help resolve issues important to local and national government, our way of life, and our cultural and ethical philosophies.

Many schools and colleges have debate teams that compete with teams from other schools, much like sports teams do. The participants travel, make friends, and meet interesting people. They also gain skills in speech, respectful listening, in-depth research, critical thinking, and evaluating information.

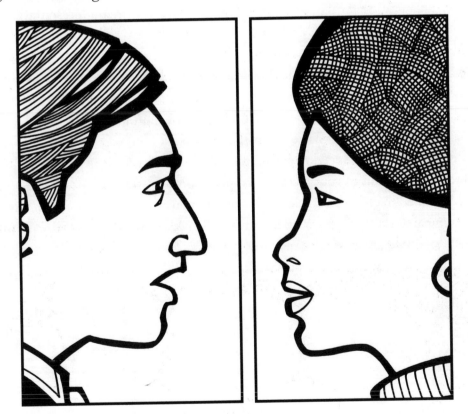

Tips for Discussions and Debates

Are you nervous when you speak in front of a group? Do you pause a lot while you are trying to speak? Do your limbs shake? Does your mouth become dry? Do you slouch, speak too softly or loudly or too quickly or slowly, or in a monotone?

Many people experience these symptoms of "stage fright." If they sound familiar to you, you might get some help from the suggestions below.

- Research the topic so you can talk more easily about it.
- Practice expressing your ideas and thoughts until you feel comfortable doing so.
- Talk about the topic with your family and friends.
- Use a mirror to get an idea of how you look when speaking. You can even practice making eye contact with the audience—your own image in the mirror.
- Use a tape recorder to help identify speech habits you would like to change and to study your voice, your phrasing, and the content of what you have to say.
- Outline your speech on a few sheets of paper or on index cards. Refer to your outline if you forget an idea. (Referring to notes is fine, as long as you don't read them word for word.)

The following suggestions will help you make a clear and convincing presentation:

- Speak slowly and clearly.
- Avoid speaking in a monotone. Vary the tone and level of your voice as you speak.
- Make eye contact with your audience.
- Stand straight for easier breathing and better voice projection.
- Use your hands to emphasize important points.
- When you are introduced to speak, take three breaths to settle yourself down before you get out of your chair. Then pause before you start speaking.
- Be prepared to answer questions that others may raise about what you have said.
- Listen carefully to what others are saying. Mark or make notes of the points you wish to answer, discuss, or question.
- Show your enthusiasm and personality.

8

Basic Rules for Discussions and Debates

Here are some basic rules for participating in discussions and debates. Your teacher and classmates may think of other rules that will help make a discussion or debate interesting and productive.

- Only one person should speak at a time. Do not interrupt the speaker. Your teacher may ask you to raise your hand if you want to contribute something.
- Some discussions and debates are moderated. Either a teacher or a student can serve as discussion leader.
- Be courteous. Do not roll your eyes, groan, or otherwise show disrespect.
- Avoid monopolizing the discussion.
- Learn to listen to others.
- Don't be afraid to voice your opinion if you disagree with what someone says.

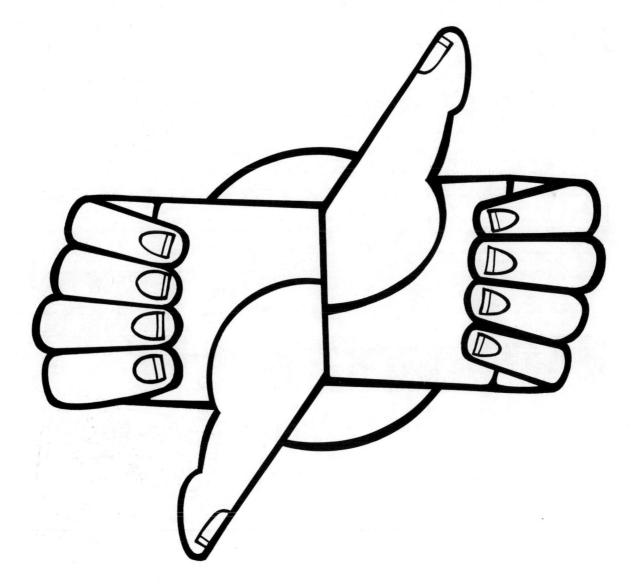

Types of Discussions

The open exchange of views is fundamental to a democratic society. One of the best places to learn this is in the classroom during a discussion or debate. This is where you get practice in speaking and being a respectful listener to diverse opinions. Talking in a group helps you learn to organize your thoughts and present them coherently. You come to see that there are several ways of looking at any issue.

Discussions can be as casual as sharing ideas with a classmate, or as formal as an organized discussion in a large group. A student or teacher can lead a discussion from the front of the class, with or without a podium, or everyone can sit in a large circle or around a table. Several small group discussions may take place at one time. If so, consider having a recorder take notes for each group and share the ideas with the entire class at the end of the discussion period.

Here are some basic guidelines for holding a discussion:

- Set some basic rules for the discussion.
- Begin by presenting the topic plainly and discussing the facts surrounding the topic.
- Question one another, ask for clarification and justification, and challenge statements or opinions.
- Defend your own opinions, or suggest alternate ideas.
- Evaluate the discussion and describe why it was useful or important.

Types of Debates

There are many ways to hold a debate in a classroom setting. Although it is not necessary to adhere to strict debate rules, you might want to use some of the terminology of a formal debate. For example:

> The _affirmative_ side of a debate supports the proposition.
> The _negative_ side of a debate opposes the proposition.
> _Constructives_ are speeches used to build arguments for the affirmative or the negative side.
> _Rebuttals_ are speeches that present evidence against an opposing view or solidify the position taken by one side. There are affirmative rebuttals and negative rebuttals.

Below are examples of several ways to conduct a debate. Be creative in the way you format your debate so that it fits your classroom setting and learning style; it does not have to conform to the directions given in these examples.

Debate Skirmish (35 to 45 minutes)
- Select an issue that interests you and other students.
- Form two teams with two people on each team. One team will be the affirmative team, and the other team will be the negative team.
- Take 10 to 15 minutes before the debate to have a general discussion about both sides of the topic. Write important points on the board. During this time, the two teams can formulate their ideas and strategies. After the discussion, give the teams a few minutes to think of what arguments they will use.

Format of the debate:
> First affirmative speaker (2 to 3 minutes)
> First negative speaker (2 to 3 minutes)
> Second affirmative speaker (2 to 3 minutes)
> Second negative speaker (2 to 3 minutes)
> Questions for both sides from the audience or from each other (10 minutes)
> Concluding negative speech (2 to 3 minutes)
> Concluding affirmative speech (2 to 3 minutes)

- One member of each team will give the first affirmative (or negative) speech and the concluding speech, and the other team member will give the second affirmative (or negative) speech.
- Evaluate the debate. If appropriate, let the audience vote on its opinions of the topic, or on the performances of the debate teams.

Partner Debate (15 to 30 minutes)

- Select an issue or topic.
- Work with a partner who has been researching the position opposite to your own.
- Debate with your partner. Create your own format, or use the guidelines for a "debate skirmish."
- Pair up with another team. As one team debates, the other team should listen and evaluate the debate. Set an appropriate time limit for each speaker based upon the amount of time available.
- Participate in a class discussion about the debates. Focus on the information that was presented in the debates. Discuss the positions, justification for each position, and recommendations about the issue.

Town Meeting (15 to 20 minutes)

This type of debate is modeled after the old-fashioned town meeting which is still popular today in Vermont. Select a topic and prepare by researching and discussing it. Appoint a moderator who will lead the meeting. Participants should raise their hands to be called on to come to the front of the room, introduce themselves, and make short speeches in support or opposition to various views of the topic. Encourage everyone to speak, and continue the meeting until everyone has had a chance to do so. Evaluate the meeting, and take a poll of the opinions of the audience.

Formal Debate (about one hour)

Formal debates are usually between two persons, with one taking the affirmative side and the other taking the negative side. However, teams can vary in size, with a different team member delivering each speech.

Format:

- First affirmative constructive (8 minutes) This is the only speech that is entirely scripted and read verbatim. This speech presents the topic and advocates an opinion or a course of action to solve the problems it raises.
- First negative constructive (8 minutes) This speech outlines the major negative positions of the affirmative case.
- Second affirmative constructive (8 minutes) This speech answers the negative arguments and is the last opportunity to submit new affirmative arguments.
- Second negative constructive (8 minutes) This is a chance to challenge the affirmative arguments and expand on one or more major negative positions.
- First negative rebuttal (5 minutes) This is the first rebuttal and challenges the second affirmative constructive.
- First affirmative rebuttal (5 minutes) Answers negative arguments already presented.
- Second negative rebuttal (5 minutes) The final speech for the negative should summarize one or more major arguments explaining why the negative side should win the debate. The negative side must satisfy the judge that the affirmative plan is not relevant to the topic or an unnecessary or unwise course of action.
- Second affirmative rebuttal (5 minutes) This is the final speech of the debate. The speaker must dispute the arguments of the negative side's final rebuttal, demonstrating the logic and benefits of the affirmative case.

SCRAM

CONTROVERSY

KAZAKHSTAN

I'LL FIGHT FOR MY RIGHTS

School Uniforms

What's the Issue?

The clothing we wear sends messages to those around us. According to sociologists, experts who study human social behavior, clothing choices reflect our cultural heritage, hobbies and occupations, religion, and values and attitudes. We recognize doctors, baseball players, scouts, religious leaders, and others by the clothing they wear. We can make political statements with our clothing, either directly, for instance by wearing a T-shirt with a controversial inscription, or indirectly, as when Mahatma Gandhi switched from wearing Western-style clothing to wearing the loincloth of the Indian peasant. The ways people decorate themselves also send messages. Earrings, hats, hair styles, tattoos, and makeup say something about those who wear them. A person's clothing can make others feel friendly, curious, fearful, or even hateful toward the person.

A growing number of educators and parents think it is a good idea to avoid the statements made by wearing certain types of clothing. The best way to do this, they feel, is to require students to wear uniforms. Wearing a uniform to school may not be so unusual for students who attend private, religious, or military schools; but, generally, American public school children have not worn uniforms.

Not everyone agrees with the proposal for mandatory uniforms, and this difference of opinion has stirred up quite a controversy among parents, school officials, and students.

15

HISTORICAL DRESS REGULATIONS

Throughout history, rulers and governments have imposed dress regulations upon groups of people for various political, religious, or economic reasons. Some examples include:

- In China, aristocratic women's feet were bound, making it impossible for the women to walk far.

- In Russia, Czar Peter the Great required his princes to shave off their beards.

- In Turkey, laws were passed in 1925 banning the fez and requiring Panama hats to be worn.

- In Iran, following the Islamic revolution in the late 1970s, laws that allowed Western customs and clothing were replaced by ones that enforced traditional Islamic codes of dress and behavior.

- The Roman Republic ruled in 215 B.C. that women could not wear more than half an ounce of gold.

- In Florence, in 1322, rulers forbade the wearing of silk and scarlet cloth by its citizens outside their houses.

- In England, Edward III ruled in 1337 that no one below the rank of knight could wear fur.

- In England, Edward III ruled that plowmen, shepherds, cowherds, dairymen, and farm laborers were to wear only russet cloth and undyed blanket cloth. Only lords might wear cloth of gold and sable furs.

- In Afganistan during the Taliban regime, Hindus were required to wear yellow badges on their chests.

16

People in favor of school uniforms argue that the choices of clothing students make—such as various styles of blue jeans, gang-related attire, Army surplus outfits, or clothing exposing midriffs—can be distractions in the classroom. Gang-related clothing is a serious problem in some schools and often intimidates other students. Supporters of uniforms argue that uniforms would help make campuses safer.

People in favor of uniforms feel that uniforms create a better learning environment, one in which learning is taken more seriously. Uniforms improve discipline, discourage cliques, and eliminate rivalry and jealousy between students. Moreover, uniforms promote school identity and spirit.

On the other hand, people opposed to school uniforms feel that poor discipline in the classroom is the result of a boring curriculum that doesn't meet the needs and interests of students. They do not feel that a change in clothing will result in better behaved students. Uniforms, they argue, would only make schools more regimented.

Proponents of school uniforms believe that requiring students to wear uniforms will improve academic performance. They cite the results of several studies that show a drop in suspensions and vandalism and an increase in attendance and grades. However, other studies have concluded that requiring students to wear uniforms has no direct effect on behavioral problems or attendance. In fact, in one study, students who were required to wear uniforms scored lower on standardized achievements tests than a comparable group of students not required to wear them.

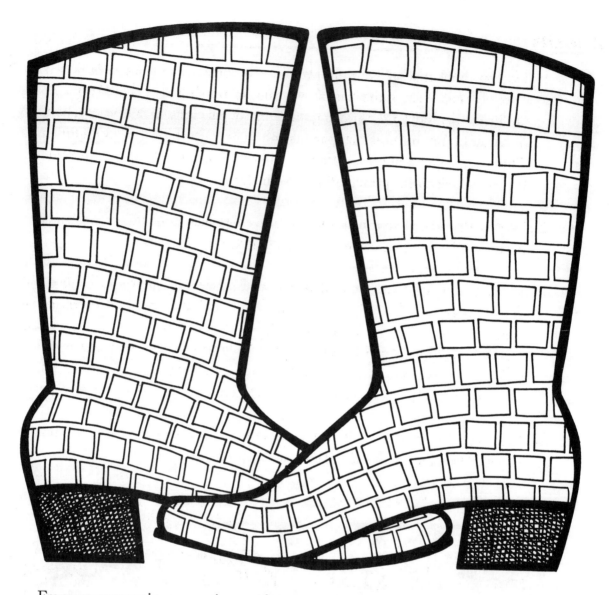

From an economic perspective, uniforms save parents enormous amounts of time and money in shopping for children's clothes. Also, uniforms can disguise the difference in economic status between students. Some teachers note, however, that adopting uniforms does not necessarily blur the socioeconomic lines at school. Wealthier students may wear all of the uniform accessories, buy the most expensive uniform components, and add designer jewelry and shoes. Less wealthy students wear only the basic uniform.

Also of concern to some people are the problems that arise when religious requirements conflict with school dress codes. Some people feel that even if schools allow head coverings or jewelry specific to a religion, they could expose students to ridicule.

Many people opposed to school uniforms argue that the United States is a diverse community and that we must respect cultural differences. Similarly, some people point out that dress is one of the few forms of self-expression that students possess. They affirm that students should have the right to read, write, speak, think, *and dress* as they please, so long as it does not interfere with education.

18

Activities

1. Do you think that school uniforms are appropriate for your school or school district? Make a list of the reasons why your school should or should not require uniforms. Consider the various groups and populations within your school or district and the concerns that parents and students in those groups might have. Then prepare an oral presentation on either the affirmative or negative side of the issue. Deliver the presentation to your class.

2. Write a diary entry that tells about your feelings and thoughts—real or imaginary—on the rule that you must wear a uniform to school.

3. Imagine that you have been hired to design school uniforms for the boys and girls at your school. Design a uniform for either boys or girls that you think would appeal to most students. Include design elements that allow for some creativity on the part of the wearer. Label the various components and accessories and write a description of the uniform. If time permits, also design a hat, scarf, or backpack coordinated with your design.

4. State your opinion on whether or not the following accessories should be banned from your school. Explain your reasoning.
    a. cross, star, or crescent necklaces
    b. burka or head coverings
    c. black lipstick
    d. yarmulkes
    e. leis or corsages
    f. pierced tongues
    g. mohawk haircuts
    h. baseball caps
    i. tattoos

5. Refer to the list "Disciplinary Problems" below. Make a list of the most pressing disciplinary problems you see in your school. Explain how uniforms could help solve some of these issues.

6. Debate whether or not schools should require students to wear uniforms. (Use the "Tips for Discussions and Debates" on page 8.)

7. Refer to the list "Historical Dress Regulations" on page 16.
   a. Identify two or three other periods of history in which a government imposed dress regulations upon a group of people.
   b. Every culture has its own standards of beauty. For example, the ancient Maya valued a flattened forehead and had a special procedure for changing the shape of an infant's head. Write an essay about some of the things people do to change the appearance of their bodies. Some examples are tattooing, body piercing, plastic surgery, and working out in a gym.

DISCIPLINARY PROBLEMS

In 1940 and 1990, public school teachers ranked the top seven disciplinary problems at public schools. Here is a comparative glance at the two lists.

1940	1990
Talking out of turn	Drug abuse
Chewing gum	Alcohol abuse
Making noise	Pregnancy
Running in the hall	Suicide
Cutting in line	Rape
Dress code violations	Robbery
Littering	Assault

20

1. Read the article titled "Tinker v. Des Moines." In your own words, explain how the First Amendment does or doesn't protect students' freedom of expression at school with regard to the following:

Hair length	Hair color
Dress codes	Body piercing
Protest armbands and/or pins	

2. If you had been a judge at the time of Tinker v. Des Moines, what would your opinion have been on the final decision? Write a note to other judges outlining how you came to your decision.

3. Imagine that you are the host of a radio talk show that specializes in controversial subjects and that you have invited a school board member, a student body president, the owner of a school uniform store, and a parent to be guests on your show. Assign four students the roles of these guests, and tell them to think about the opinions they would have on school uniforms. Create a list of questions to ask the guests that will stimulate discussion. Present your radio show in front of a live audience, or tape record the show.

THE CASE OF TINKER ET AL. V. DES MOINES

John F. Tinker, Christopher Eckhardt, and Mary Beth Tinker attended public schools in Des Moines, Iowa. They decided to publicize their opposition to the Vietnam War by wearing black armbands. The principals of the Des Moines schools became aware of the plan and on December 14, 1965, adopted a policy prohibiting students from wearing armbands while at school. Refusal to remove the armband would result in suspension. On December 16 and 17, Mary Beth, John, Christopher, and several other students wore the black armbands to their schools in defiance of the new policy. They were all sent home and suspended from school until they removed the armbands. A complaint was filed in U.S. District Court stating that the students' right of free expression had been violated.

In *Tinker v. Des Moines* the court ruled that this type of expression was close to being "pure speech." Since the school officials had not shown that the conduct had materially and substantially interfered with the discipline of the school, it was protected under the First Amendment, and all punishment by the school district had to be rescinded. The students had been quiet and passive. They were not disruptive and did not infringe upon the rights of others. A prohibition against expression of opinion that doesn't lead to substantial interference with school discipline or the rights of others is not permissible under the First and Fourteenth Amendments.

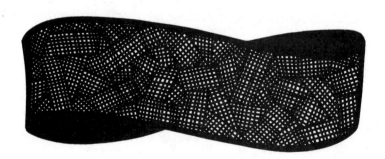

22

TOPIC #2

Bullying

What's the Issue?

Bullying—when someone keeps doing or saying things in order to have power over you—can be very annoying or even frightening. Bullies use many methods to intimidate others. Some of them are:

- calling people names
- saying or writing nasty things about others
- leaving others out of activities
- not talking to others
- threatening people
- making people feel uncomfortable or scared
- taking or damaging other people's belongings
- hitting or kicking people
- making people do things they don't want to do

Why do some people bully others? Some see bullying as a way of being popular or making themselves look tough and in charge. Some do it to get attention or to make other people afraid of them. Others are jealous of the people they are bullying.

Some young people are bullied for no apparent reason, but sometimes it's because they are different in some way—perhaps it's the color of their skin, the way they talk, their clothing styles or an unusual name. Sometimes young people are bullied because they look as though they won't stand up for themselves.

Most students, parents, and educators are very concerned about bullying. At issue is whether or not there should be school regulations against bullying, and whether a zero-tolerance policy should be adopted. (Zero tolerance means that any type of misbehavior is unacceptable, and subject to mandatory punishment.)

People in favor of zero-tolerance anti-bullying regulations on school campuses argue that being bullied is not good for young people. It can make them feel lonely, unhappy, and frightened. They can lose confidence and may not want to go to school anymore. A policy of zero-tolerance toward bullying increases sense of organization and enhances social bonding among students.

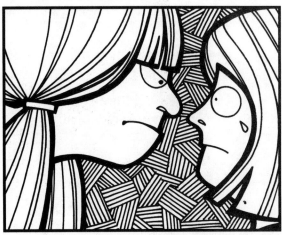

Advocates claim that if there were zero tolerance on campus, students who witnessed bullying incidents would be more likely to speak up about it. In addition, adults would have to take complaints about bullying seriously; zero tolerance would force teachers to intervene.

According to proponents, anti-bullying campaigns do make a difference—in some schools where strict policies have been adopted, bullying has dropped by 50 percent.

People opposed to anti-bullying regulations and zero tolerance cite studies that show that zero tolerance doesn't teach kids better behavior; it just makes them bitter. It is based on a criminal model, not an educational one, and educators end up treating children who make mistakes as though they were criminals. Opponents ask whether something that can be handled in the principal's office should be a reason for suspension.

Some people think bullying is just part of growing up and a way for young people to learn to stick up for themselves. Should staring, rolling your eyes at a comment, or giving dirty looks count as punishable behavior? Where should the line be drawn? There must be an opportunity for people who make mistakes—especially children—to make amends.

1. Imagine that you have been instrumental in creating a community in which the problem of bullying has been solved. Pretend that you and two or three other students are members of the community's city council and that you have been asked to explain to educators and government officials how your system works. Draw up a list of the rules that your community uses. Make an oral presentation describing your policies and why they have been effective.

2. Do you think that you, one individual, can help solve the problems of bullying? Write a hypothetical letter to your principal or newspaper editor that explains why you do or do not think that you might be able to make a difference in people's attitudes about bullying.

3. Work with a small group of students to create a colorful poster that promotes an anti-bullying campaign.

4. Debate the topic "A student should be expelled after a first bullying offense." Use the "Tips for Discussions and Debates on" page 8.

1. Conduct interviews with your principal, teacher, parents, and classmates to get a variety of opinions on bullying and zero tolerance. Refer to the "Interview Tips" on the following page for hints on how to conduct an interview.

   Make a list of the questions that you want to ask. Some sample questions are:

   > What does or does not constitute bullying?
   > Were you ever bullied or teased? Explain.
   > What should be the punishment for bullying?
   > What is your opinion of zero tolerance?
   > Did you ever bully someone? Explain.

2. Study the interview responses. Write an article summarizing your findings. Compare and contrast your findings with others in your class. Communicate the information you gathered by presenting it to the class, the principal, or a student council meeting.

INTERVIEW TIPS

Plan the Interview

1. Set an objective for the interview. Why do you want to conduct an interview, and what do you intend to do with the information you gather?
2. Make a list of people who might have the information you're looking for.
3. Contact the people you would like to interview. Tell them about your project, and explain why you would like to interview them. Ask them when would be a convenient time for the interview, and make an appointment.

Prepare the Interview

1. Draw up a list of questions. Do some research before preparing your questions so that you will cover the issue thoroughly.
2. Use open-ended questions that encourage personal answers, such as "Tell me what you remember about going to school."

Conduct the Interview

1. Be sure to arrive on time or make your phone call at the time agreed upon.
2. Don't interrupt or attempt to correct the person you are interviewing.
3. Let the person know if you will be taping the interview.
4. Listen carefully to your subject's responses, and ask follow-up questions based on what he or she says.
5. Don't assume you know what your subject means. If he or she is vague, prompt him or her to be more specific.
6. After the interview, leave things as you found them. Be sure to send a thank you note.

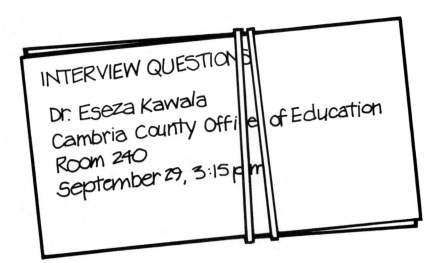

INTERVIEW QUESTIONS

Dr. Eseza Kawala
Cambria County Office of Education
Room 240
September 29, 3:15 pm

¿Qué pasa?

Should the U.S. Have an Official Language?

What's the Issue?

Many countries have official languages—languages designated by the government to be used for all official business. For example, the official language of Costa Rica is Spanish; of Greenland, Inupik; and of Haiti, French. Some countries have several official languages. English and French are the official languages of Canada, and Spanish and Quechua are the official languages of Peru.

Some countries don't have official languages. In the United States, despite the fact that most Americans speak English, there is no official language. The United States has always been a place where many languages are spoken. At the time of the nation's founding, 20 languages were commonly spoken, including Dutch, French, German, and numerous Native American languages. The Articles of Confederation were printed in German as well as English. During the nineteenth and early twentieth centuries, the nation's linguistic diversity grew as Europeans immigrated to America in growing numbers.

Several language laws have been enacted since the late nineteenth century. In 1837, Pennsylvania passed a law requiring school instruction to be in both German and English. In 1839, Ohio adopted a bilingual education law, authorizing German and English instruction at the request of a student's parent. School instruction was held in English and French in Louisiana and English and Spanish in New Mexico.

In the early 1980s, a political interest group called "English Only" sought to establish English as the nation's official language and sponsored a constitutional amendment to make it so. The Language of Government Act has been pending before the House and Senate since 1991. More than 20 states have passed various forms of English-only legislation. Some states even have laws that protect the use of languages other than English. Hawaii, for example, recognizes both English and Hawaiian as official languages.

Focus on the Controversy

If English were designated the official language of the United States, it would mean that only English would be used for government business. This includes all public documents, records, legislation, and regulations, as well as hearings, ceremonies, and public meetings. The use of languages other than English would be allowed for such things as public health and safety services, court proceedings, international trade, and foreign language instruction. The Voting Rights Act of 1965, which allows ballots and other materials to be printed in languages other than English, would be repealed.

Supporters of English as the official language argue that English is the glue that holds Americans together. It is the language of opportunity in the United States. A single common language would facilitate the assimilation of immigrants into society and prevent their isolation. English-only supporters claim that a system that accommodates immigrants in their native languages lowers the incentive to learn English and restricts immigrants to low-skilled, low-paying jobs. English advocates point out that an official language policy would in no way affect what languages are spoken in a person's home.

Those opposed to declaring English an official language say it's unnecessary to have an official language, since English is not threatened. For two centuries, most immigrant groups have learned English within a generation without any laws compelling them to do so. Current immigrants are doing the same. An English law would perpetuate false stereotypes of immigrants and promote hostility toward non-English speakers.

Opponents argue that an official-language law would discourage bilingual programs that help students build on their linguistic skills. Prohibiting or discouraging diversity in language limits learning opportunities, they say. Also, making English the official language of the United States would raise Constitutional concerns. The First Amendment guarantees freedom of speech. The Fourteenth Amendment forbids abridging the privileges and immunities of naturalized citizens. English-only laws violate these constitutional rights, say opponents.

Opponents to an official language believe that the bond that unites our nation is not language or ethnicity, but a shared commitment to democracy, liberty, and equality.

1. Take a survey of the different languages that are spoken in your classroom or school. Make a bar graph to illustrate the number of speakers of each language.

2. Do you agree with the statement "English is the language of opportunity in America?" Explain your opinion in a short paragraph. Include a list of the opportunities that you think could be missed by a person who is not fluent in English.

3. Write a letter to an imaginary immigrant family giving advice from your perspective on what they might do when they arrive in America to make the transition to a new culture easier. Include information and handy hints about schools, jobs, recreation, shopping, and learning English.

4. Debate the topic "English should be America's official language." Use the "Tips for Discussions and Debates" on page 8.

5. America has been described as both a "melting pot" and a "salad bowl." What two different concepts are represented by these images? Write a short description of these metaphors. Then write a poem or story, create a collage or poster, or draw a picture that illustrates the metaphor you think best describes the American people.

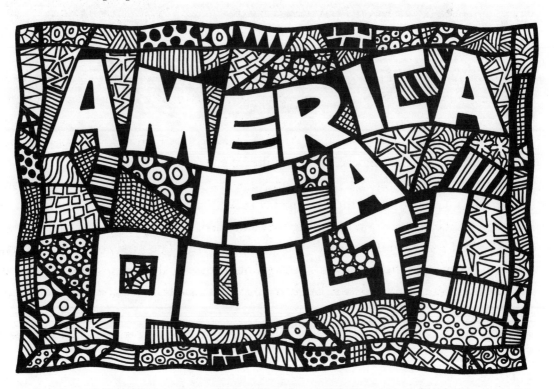

Extended Activities

1. Do research on the Internet or in the library to learn more about Frederick A.C. Muhlenberg and find other versions of this story (see page 34). What features do various versions of the story have in common, and how do they differ? Write a short explanation of what you think probably really happened.

2. Imagine that the year is 1795 and you are a journalist covering the U.S. House of Representatives during the proceedings mentioned in the Muhlenberg legend. Write a newspaper article describing the details of the proceedings. Pretend that you are able to interview Muhlenberg and others involved, and use "quotes" from them in your story.

3. If the proposal to have laws issued in German as well as in English had passed, what differences do you think you would you see in America today? Write a short essay describing these differences.

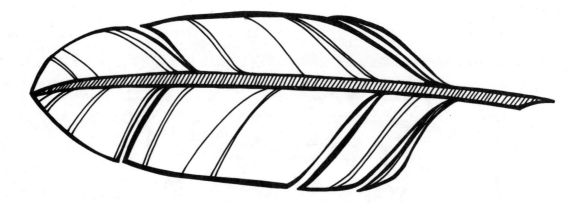

4. The Muhlenberg legend (see page 34) has been around since at least the time of the Civil War, and was initially spread by people celebrating German contributions to American culture. The story is used today by some English-only supporters to demonstrate how easy it might be for another language, like Spanish, to become the nation's official language. Do you think this is a legitimate fear? In a short paragraph, explain why or why not.

5. In 1751, Benjamin Franklin wrote, "Why should Pennsylvania, founded by the English, become a Colony of Aliens, who will shortly be so numerous as to Germanize us instead of our Anglifying them, and will never adopt our Language or Customs, any more than they can acquire our Complexion?"

   Write an essay about Franklin's statement in which you discuss what was happening in American in 1751 when Franklin made this statement and whether or not Franklin's opinion is valid in the United States today.

THE MUHLENBERG LEGEND

The Muhlenberg legend is a story popularized after the Civil War, about the time when the German language nearly became the official language of the United States. Little evidence exists to prove that this story is really true; nevertheless, it continues to survive in many versions. According to one popular version, in 1795 a group of Virginia Germans petitioned to have certain laws issued in German as well as in English. There was some discussion about which language to adopt, with some ardent separatists arguing that English was the language of the "enemy," and therefore to be shunned. The proposal was defeated by one vote, apparently cast by Frederick A.C. Muhlenberg, a Pennsylvania German who served as the first Speaker of the U.S. House of Representatives. However, it was clear from the start that most people considered changing from English to German to be too much trouble.

34

Religion in Schools

What's the Issue?

Religious freedom is one of the most important traditions and constitutional rights we have in the United States. Most people agree with this, yet many public school officials must confront the issue of whether or not prayer and other forms of religious observance should be allowed at their schools.

The opening two clauses of the First Amendment deal with the issue of what the government can and cannot do with respect to religion: "Congress shall make no law respecting an establishment of religion, or prohibiting the free exercise thereof...."

The first of these clauses is called the Establishment Clause and many events and circumstances led to its adoption. It guarantees the separation of religion from government. Before the First Amendment was written, most states had officially established churches, including the Congregational Church in New England and the Anglican Church in the South. These denominations often persecuted the members of various minority religions who were denied the right to hold public office and were required to pay taxes to support the established church. By the time the Constitution was framed, many people felt strongly about the separation of church and state. Thomas Jefferson wrote of the need for a "wall of separation between church and state."

In 1971, a Supreme Court ruling, *Lemon v. Kurtzman*, established a three-part test for determining whether a law or policy has breached the wall between church and state. The Lemon test asks:

Does the law or policy have a secular purpose?

Does the law or policy advance or endorse religion?

Does the law or policy foster excessive entanglement between the state and religion?

If the answer to any of these questions is yes, then the law or policy violates the Establishment Clause of the First Amendment.

"[Or] prohibiting the free exercise thereof," is called the Free Exercise Clause. It prohibits the government from interfering with individuals' rights to worship as they choose, in most instances. The roots of the Free Exercise Clause reach back to the country's colonial period, when intolerance threatened religious minorities' freedom of worship. For example, Roger Williams founded Rhode Island in 1644 as a haven for religious minorities including Anabaptists, Quakers, and Jews.

Throughout the years, the Supreme Court has had to resolve conflicting interpretations of the First Amendment. The issue of prayer in public schools was raised in the 1830s when waves of Italian and Irish Catholic immigrants came to this country and objected to Protestant prayers and Bible readings. There were bitter conflict, riots, and even some deaths over the issue. Intolerance has also occasionally threatened freedom of worship, and in the 1940s the Supreme Court began interpreting whether a particular policy or law violated the First Amendment with respect to religion. In 1962, the controversy over state-mandated or state-sponsored prayer in public schools was debated in the Supreme Court (Engel v. Vitale), and the Court ruled that such observances violate the Establishment Clause.

36

Opponents to prayer in school point out that more than fifty years of Supreme Court rulings have maintained the separation of church and state based on the principles that public schools may not take sides in matters of religion and may not endorse a particular religion or any religion at all.

Proponents of prayer in school say that the founding fathers never intended the separation of church and state, but that the Establishment Clause was intended to bar only the establishment of a state religion. They contend that our government is based on religious principles, pointing out that Congress prays at the opening of every session, that "In God We Trust" appears on our currency, and that the Pledge of Allegiance includes the words "under God." They wonder why religion and prayer are accepted in government institutions, but not in school.

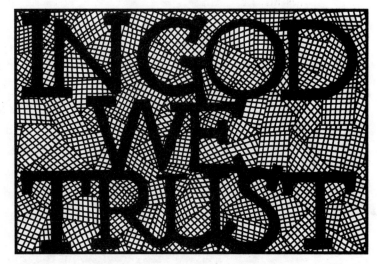

Those in favor of prayer in school also assert that the restriction of student-led prayer violates students' First Amendment right to practice religion without government interference. However, opponents to prayer in school contend that it is sponsored prayer in the classroom that undermines the religious freedom clauses of the First Amendment. Prayer is a religious exercise, so school supported prayer amounts to the establishment of a religious practice and is therefore unconstitutional. It also violates the Free Exercise Clause by exposing students to prayer against their will or forcing them to leave class in order to avoid hearing prayers, opponents claim.

Another argument in support of school prayer is based on the perception that our country is in moral decline. Divorce, teen pregnancy, violent crime, and drug abuse have all increased, and advocates of school prayer maintain that there is a direct correlation between the removal of prayer from public schools and the decline of public morality. Opponents of school prayer find no evidence that prayer improves morality. Instead, they claim that the country's social problems are due to poverty, inequality, and lack of opportunity.

It is interesting to note that, despite this controversy, the First Amendment does guarantee every child the right to pray in school voluntarily. Other religious activities are permitted in public schools as long as the state plays no role in organizing them, and as long as they do not disrupt the educational mission of the school. For example, some current laws hold that:

- Students have the right to pray individually or in groups or to discuss their religious views with their peers so long as they are not disruptive. However, this does not give students the right to a captive audience, or to compel other students to participate.

- Students may be taught *about* religion in classes on comparative religions and history of religion, but public schools may not teach religion.

- Religious messages on T-shirts and the like are protected free speech. Students may wear religious attire such as yarmulkes and head scarves, and may not be forced to wear gym clothes that they regard as immodest, on religious grounds.

- Students may express their religious beliefs in the form of reports, homework, and artwork, and such expressions are constitutionally protected.

- Public schools may teach about religious holidays and their religious aspects, but may observe only secular aspects of holidays. They may not observe holidays as religious events.

1. Work with a partner to write a simpler, clearer version of the First Amendment that would help eliminate controversy over religion in public schools.

2. With a small group of students create a class mural that depicts the historical context of the First Amendment as it pertains to religion.

3. Pretend you are a judge who must hear four cases involving religion in public school settings. Your job is to analyze the cases and then decide on whether or not to allow the disputed activities to continue. Write a short summary of your decisions outlining the reasons for your positions.
   Case 1: A group of students wear emblems to identify their religious affiliation.
   Case 2: Several teachers assign projects on world religions.
   Case 3: Two students write stories about attending a religious summer camp.
   Case 4: Each morning a teacher leads her class in prayer.
   Case 5: A room in a public high school is set aside for students to hold prayer sessions throughout the school day.

4. Debate whether or not prayers should be allowed in public schools. (Use "Tips for Discussions and Debates" on page 8.)

1. Work with a group of students to analyze the case of Abington School District v. Schempp (below). Create a "friend of the court" brief that includes the following information:

    a. An overview of the case, highlighting what happened, the parties involved, and the important facts.

    b. The arguments for and against both the Abington School district and the Schempp family.

    c. A summary of your group's decision on the case, and a summary of the actual Supreme Court decision.

2. Present your brief to the class, using charts to clarify important points.

ABINGTON SCHOOL DISTRICT V. SCHEMPP (1963)

Summary

In 1958, the Pennsylvania legislature passed a law directing that at least ten verses from the Bible be read at the beginning of each school day. The law was amended in 1959 to allow children to be excused from the readings with a written request from a parent or guardian. At Abington High School, in Abington Township, the verses were read over the intercom system. The students were also asked to stand and repeat the Lord's Prayer. The students had the option of leaving the room, or remaining without participating. The law was challenged by the Schempp family.

Cloning

What's the Issue?

In 1997, a little lamb—now more famous than Mary's little lamb—made headlines. She was named Dolly and by all appearances she looked like a very ordinary lamb. But the way she was born was very extraordinary. She was famous because she was the very first lamb cloned from cells from another sheep.

Cloning is the part of genetic engineering in which scientists use a variety of methods to create an exact copy of a living being. To make a clone, a cell from a donor animal is grown inside a host female. The host then gives birth to a cloned baby animal. This offspring doesn't have any of the qualities of its "mother." It is an exact copy, or clone, of the donor animal.

Following the birth of Dolly, other scientists created five pig clones using genetic material taken from a body cell of an adult female pig. Scientists have also cloned cows and mice. A number of scientists and other people believe it is only a matter of time before human cloning becomes a reality.

There was a huge reaction to the announcement of Dolly's birth from the media, scientists, and lawmakers. Most of the concern was about human cloning, but it was also about cloning in general. President Bill Clinton imposed a ban on the use of government funds for cloning research, and Pope John Paul II issued a statement insisting that each human being had a right to unique human genes. UNESCO issued its Universal Declaration on the Human Genome, banning the reproductive cloning of human beings. And on January 18, 2002, a National Academy of Sciences panel said that cloning was unsafe and should be outlawed, though it advocated cloning embryos to treat diseases. President George W. Bush, however, opposed cloning for any purpose. People on both sides of the issue continue to debate the scientific, social, and ethical ramifications of cloning.

Focus on the Controversy

Many of the important arguments in favor of cloning have to do with solving human medical problems. For example, skin for burn victims, brain cells for people with brain damage, and spinal cord cells for paraplegics and quadriplegics could be produced by cloning. Hearts, lungs, livers, and kidneys could be produced for people who need organ transplants. Opponents of cloning are afraid that humans would be cloned just for the purpose of harvesting organs. Proponents, however, point out that entire humans wouldn't have to be cloned—only the organs themselves would have to be cloned.

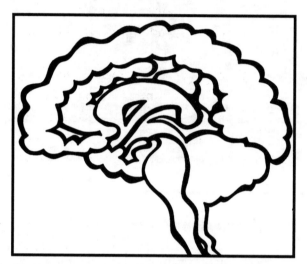

In addition to providing replacement organs, cloning may also help cure conditions such as Alzheimer's disease, Parkinson's disease, cystic fibrosis, diabetes, heart failure, degenerative joint diseases like rheumatism, and leukemia. Also, infertile couples could use cloning to have children who are biologically related to them. Cloning could also be used to produce animals who carry human genes that produce proteins useful in the manufacture of drugs.

The objections to cloning, say its proponents, are similar to objections to previous scientific achievements, such as heart transplantation and in vitro fertilization, that later came to be widely accepted.

Many people opposed to cloning are concerned that tampering with nature would have disastrous consequences. Cloning, they say, could lead to the creation of bizarre, if not dangerous, new life forms. At the very least, the introduction of clones has the potential to upset the balance of life as we now know it. There is also some fear that cloning would lead to the creation of genetically engineered groups of people for specific purposes, such as warfare or menial labor.

There are also concerns about the safety of cloning. There are still too many unknown factors that could adversely affect cloned animals or people, say opponents. There will be need for many rules and regulations, and it seems like an overwhelming job to legislate cloning.

42

Other concerns about cloning focus on religious and philosophical beliefs. Opponents feel that some aspects of human life should be off limits to science. To them, cloning a person violates basic human dignity and destroys a person's uniqueness, and many people believe that cloning is at odds with the traditional concept of family.

Activities

1. In the movie *Jurassic Park*, living dinosaurs were cloned from samples taken from DNA trapped in ancient amber. Pretend you are a screenwriter for a major motion picture company. Write a description of a movie script that is based on cloning and that you feel will be a box office hit.

2. Six months after the National Bioethics Advisory Commission called for a legal ban on human cloning for three to five years, a physicist named Richard Seed announced that he was looking for partners to open a human cloning clinic. Write an editorial on the topic of human cloning. Include your opinion of the work of Richard Seed and whether or not he should be allowed to continue with his research.

3. To better understand different perspectives on cloning, write a diary entry for each of the people listed below. Include details of an imaginary incident involving cloning and the person's feelings and emotions surrounding the incident.
   - a genetic engineer
   - a person who needs an organ transplant
   - a pharmaceutical salesman
   - a religious leader

4. Prepare a late-breaking special report story for a local radio station on the topic of cloning. Include these words in the news story: gene, DNA, genetics, bioethics.

5. Write a newspaper editorial expressing one of the following opinions:
   - Human cloning is a good idea.
   - Human cloning is too risky at this point and should not be attempted until further research has been done.
   - Human cloning should never be attempted.

·THE LEGEND OF·
DITTO
THE GREAT DUPLICATOR

6. Debate the proposition "Cloning is too difficult to legislate, so it should never be attempted." For suggestions on how to organize a discussion or debate, refer to "Tips for Discussions and Debates" on page 8.

7. Make a collage that illustrates how technology has influenced the course of history. You might include pictures (or your own drawings) of automobiles, televisions, computers, or cloning technologies.

8. A myth is a story that tries to explain the mysterious or unknown, such as natural phenomena, puzzling events, or the actions of people. These stories were usually invented by people who did not understand what was going on around them, and tried to explain what they saw by creating myths. Imagine that you have just arrived from a place that never heard of cloning, and, in your attempt to understand this puzzling event, you decide to write a myth. First, decide what aspect of cloning you want to explain. Next, decide what gods, heroes, creatures, or animals will appear in your story. Give them names and personalities. Then write your myth, and include one or two illustrations.

44

1. Work with a small group of students to put together a project called "The Historical Trail to Dolly." This can be an essay, scrapbook, poster, or mural. Focus on important places, people, scientific discoveries, and events. Limit the number of items you research to about ten. Use the information in the chart "Steps Leading to the Cloning of Dolly," interviews with experts, and other reference materials.

2. In the book *Frankenstein* by Mary Wollstonecraft Shelley, Victor Frankenstein took body parts from various cadavers in dissecting rooms and elsewhere and assembled them into a new body. Mary Shelley took her story's ideas about the nature of life from some of Europe's top scientists and thinkers, and her premise from experiments that had tried to use electricity to restore life to the recently dead. Mary Shelley was silent on just how Victor Frankenstein imparted life to his creation, saying only that success crowned "days and nights of incredible labor and fatigue."

   • Would you consider Frankenstein's monster a clone? Explain your reasoning in a short paragraph.

   • Some people contend that cloning of humans will create monsters. Do your own research to determine the possibility of creating cloned monsters. Write a short speech arguing either side of this opinion and present it to the class.

   • Learn more about Shelley's novel and the movies based on it. Begin at the National Library of Medicine Web site: http://www.nlm.nih.gov/hmd/frankenstein/frankhome.html. Then work with a partner to create your own imaginative story based on the modern science of cloning.

STEPS LEADING TO THE CLONING OF DOLLY

1952   The first animal cloning occurs when Robert Briggs and Thomas King create frogs from tadpole cells.

1953   James Watson and Francis Crick discover the double helix structure of DNA. They are awarded the Nobel prize in physiology in 1962.

1962   John Gurdon clones frogs, this time using cells from older tadpoles.

1969   A Harvard Medical School team isolates the first gene.

1978   Baby Louise, the first child conceived through in vitro fertilization, is born.

1983   The first human mother-to-mother embryo transfer occurs.

1985   Ralph Brinster's lab creates the first transgenic livestock— pigs that produce a human growth hormone.

1993   Human embryos are cloned.

1997   The first cloned mammal is born—a sheep named Dolly, cloned by Ian Wilmut and a team of scientists in Scotland.

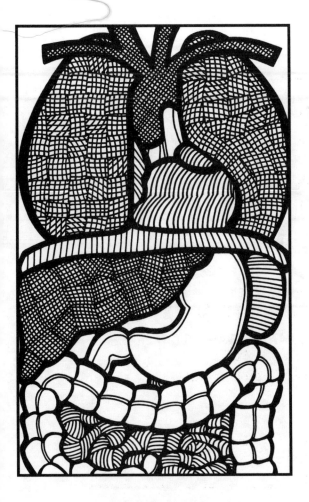

Organ Transplants

What's the Issue?

Since the first successful transplant of a kidney more than 50 years ago, organ transplantation has become almost routine. Nowadays, thanks to organ transplants, people with potentially fatal organ diseases and failures can look forward to long, healthy lives.

The problem is that there aren't enough organs to go around. According to the United Network for Organ Sharing, more than 79,000 people in the United States alone are wondering whether they will get the transplants they need to survive.

The success of organ transplantation has created many ethical questions. A central issue is whether or not current methods of allocating scarce organs is fair. Other issues involve the questions of who should decide whether or not to donate a deceased person's organs, who should be allowed to donate an organ, whether alcoholics should receive new livers, and whether donors should be paid for their organs. These questions have no easy answers and continue to be the subject of public controversy.

UNITED NETWORK FOR ORGAN SHARING NATIONAL PATIENT WAITING LIST

Kidney transplant	51,544
Liver transplant	17,641
Pancreas transplant	1,253
Pancreas islet cell transplant	276
Kidney-pancreas transplant	2,530
Intestine transplant	179
Heart transplant	4,136
Heart-lung transplant	208
Lung transplant	3,824
Total	**79,226**

Focus on the Controversy

Is the allocation program fair?

The main controversy concerning organ transplantation is whether or not the organ allocation system is fair. In the United States, the United Network for Organ Sharing (UNOS) maintains a national waiting list for organs. In general, the sickest patients are given preference and are moved to the top of the list. The current organ allocation program is intended to be as fair and unbiased as possible, and the main goal is to allow for the most survivors.

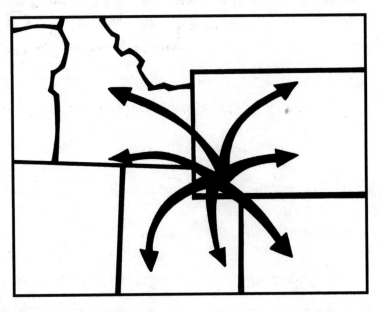

Opponents of UNOS, however, maintain that this system gives some patients an unfair advantage. For example, UNOS maintains a national list, but organs are distributed regionally whenever possible. That means patients can improve their odds by getting themselves listed at more than one transplant center. A wealthy patient who can afford to travel to several centers will probably get an organ faster than a patient who can't. People opposed to UNOS policies feel that organs should be given to the sickest patients—no matter what disease they have, how long they have had it, or where they live.

Several other UNOS policies are also controversial. One new policy excludes patients with chronic autoimmune liver diseases from top priority in receiving a liver transplant. UNOS based its policy on information that patients with chronic autoimmune diseases are poor transplant candidates. Under another policy, patients suffering from acute liver failure (a disease that is severe and quickly comes to a crisis point) get priority over those with long-term liver failure because they have a better chance of full recovery.

One UNOS representative said that they are continuing to look for a better way to allocate organs. Two options under study are a single national list, where the sickest patient who matches with the donor gets the organ no matter how far away; and the optimized single national list, in which assigned points are given for distance, waiting time, and status.

Should living people donate their organs?

A quarter of all transplanted kidneys in the United States come from living donors. Most of these come from relatives of patients who need transplants. This raises an important issue: Should living people be allowed to donate their organs? People in favor argue that the results are generally better with living-donor organs than with those obtained from cadavers.

Another advantage of so-called "dedicated donation" is that recipients don't have to wait for an organ to become available, and so the transplant can be performed as a planned procedure under optimal conditions. As an added bonus, people who can't find a match among relatives or volunteers would not have to compete for cadaver organs with as many other patients.

Opponents say that it isn't ethical to expose a healthy donor to risk for a procedure that won't benefit the donor and could cause harm. There is also great potential for psychological harm if the recipient doesn't follow good medical practices, especially if the donated organ is rejected. The donor might resent the recipient for not taking good care of his or her health. Some people wonder if either the recipient or the donor could sue under such circumstances.

Opponents are also very concerned that donations could be coerced by family members, hospital staff, or attorneys, forcing reluctant donors to make this important decision based on guilt or even bribery or blackmail.

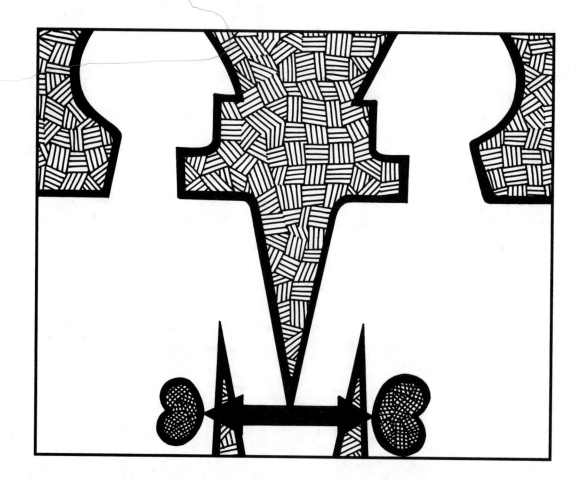

50

Should people be able to sell their organs?

The 1984 National Organ Transplant Act made selling organs illegal in the United States. Some people think this policy should be reconsidered. Offering compensation would en-

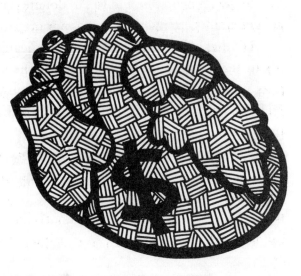

courage donations they say, increasing the number of organs available. Everyone else involved in the transplant process is compensated, and perhaps the donor or his family should be, too. People who think selling organs is a good policy argue that we live in a free-market society, and individuals should be permitted to do whatever they wish with their organs.

People opposed to compensation for organ donation argue that there is great potential for black market commerce. In some countries, black markets do exist to connect patients with donors. Desperate patients can't afford the years it takes to make their way up a waiting list, but some can afford to spend many thousands of dollars to circumvent the allocation system. This can lead to exploitation—one person taking advantage of the misfortune of another for his or her own benefit—and it also gives an advantage to the wealthy.

Who should decide whether or not a deceased person's organs are donated?

Many people feel that only the donor should make the decision to donate an organ. If a person can legally will a bank account or a car to someone, why not a heart or liver? Once the donor's decision has been made, the family should not be allowed to interfere. Some medical professionals suggest adopting a policy called "required response," under which all adults would be required to declare their preferences regarding organ donation. Their preferences would be recorded in a central database accessible to organ banks, and their wishes would be honored despite any objections from their families.

Other people argue that donors' families should participate in the decisions. They contend that a sick or dying person often can't make a careful decision, so it should be left up to the family. They also feel that a family should be able to override the decision of a deceased relative. But others argue that grieving families may be in no position to make such an important decision.

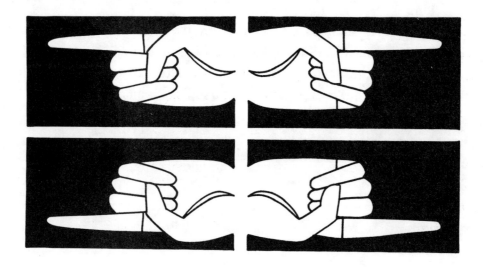

52

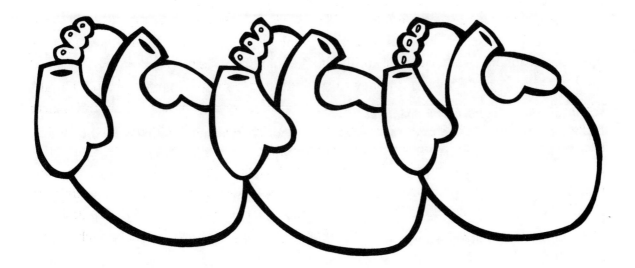

In fact, many people say that the solution to increasing the donor pool is to remove families from the decision-making process altogether. When people realize that organ donation is good for our society, they say, donations will become standard. Such a policy is called "presumed consent"—that is, no one would allow such a precious resource to be withheld after death, so it would be presumed that everyone would donate their organs. Then families wouldn't have to decide, and medical personnel wouldn't have to ask.

Opponents argue that there is already an unfounded but widespread belief that if doctors know you're a donor they won't try to save your life. "Presumed consent" would only fuel that fear, they say, creating an anti-donation backlash whereby potential donors would opt out of the system without considering the good that transplants can do.

Should alcoholics receive liver donations?

Except for the kidney, no organ is transplanted more often than the liver. In the United States, alcoholic liver disease is the most common cause of liver failure. Should patients with a history of alcoholism be treated like everyone else when organs become available? Or should we give priority to non-alcoholic patients, who are more likely to benefit from transplants?

People in favor of allowing alcoholic patients to receive new livers argue that we should place the same moral blame on people who overeat and smoke and end up needing new hearts or lungs. Personal prejudices and a view of alcoholism as a moral failing rather than a disease influence decision-making, they say.

Some transplant teams won't perform liver transplants for alcoholic patients under any circumstances. Others, following a recommendation by the UNOS, require six months of sobriety before a transplant. The cost of transplantation is higher for alcoholics because alcoholism is typically accompanied by other serious medical conditions. There is also a greater risk of relapse and graft failure in alcoholic patients.

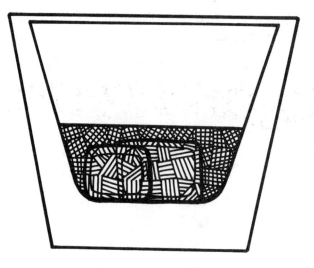

Should prisoners receive organ donations?

Early in January 2002, a California prison inmate serving time for robbery received a heart transplant, while over 4,000 other Americans were waiting for new hearts. As news of the transplant spread, the level of debate over transplants for prisoners became more heated.

A spokesman for UNOS said that he had not heard of any other case of an inmate receiving a heart transplant. The California Department of Corrections said it had to follow court rulings regarding inmate care, and cited a 1976 Supreme Court ruling that declared it "cruel and unusual punishment" to withhold necessary medical care from inmates.

Those in favor of the transplant argue that from a medical point of view, the state had no reason to deny the prisoner. He violated the law, but that did not eliminate his right to medical care. An ethics committee from Stanford University where the transplant was done approved him and put him on the waiting list, so it was strictly a medical decision.

If people oppose giving organs to prisoners, they must petition state lawmakers to change the law, according to some medical ethicists. New laws were passed after liver transplants were given to several drug addicts and alcoholics.

A BRIEF HISTORY OF TRANSPLANTS

1933   First human-to-human kidney transplant (the kidney never functioned).

1954   First successful kidney transplant, from one twin to another, with no anti-rejection drugs necessary (Dr. Joseph Murray, Brigham & Women's Hospital, Boston).

1967   First successful liver transplant (Dr. Thomas Starzl, University of Colorado Health Sciences Center, Denver).

1967   First heart transplant on a human being (Dr. Christiaan Barnard, Groote Schuur Hospital in Cape Town, South Africa).

1968   First successful heart transplant in United States (Dr. Denton Cooley, Houston's St. Luke's Episcopal Hospital).

1968   Uniform Anatomical Gift Act passed in the United States, creating the "donor card" and allowing families to consent to or refuse donation; prohibited doctors attending the donor from participating in organ removal or transplantation.

1978   Uniform Brain Death Act passed in the United States, expanding for the first time the traditional definition of death to assert "brain death" *is* death.

1983   Cyclosporine, a revolutionary anti-rejection drug, approved for commercial use, creating a huge increase in transplants.

1984   National Organ Transplant Act passed in the United States, prohibiting the sale of human organs and setting up a national network to procure and distribute organs. The United Network for Organ Sharing oversees the network.

1986   "Routine request" law passed in the United States, requiring hospitals to give families the opportunity to donate organs by asking them in appropriate cases.

56

1. Could a convict make amends for his crimes by donating a kidney or an eye? This question has been asked by people who are concerned about the fairness of transplant policies and the lack of available organs. Discuss this question with a small group of classmates. Consider both sides of the question. Then write an essay that explains your opinions on the topic.

2. Choose one of the following topics to debate. Use the "Tips for Discussions and Debates" on page 8.
    > Prisoners should be allowed to receive heart and liver transplants.
    > It should be illegal to sell one's organs.
    > Only a person's family should decide if his or her organs should be donated.

3. As the newly appointed chair of an organ transplant symposium, you must create an educational program that teaches people the importance of donating organs. Work with a partner to produce a poster, brochure, or magazine advertisement that will be part of your public education program.

4. You are a journalist. The editor of your newspaper just assigned you to a story about a child who will be undergoing an organ transplant because of the generosity of another family whose child died in an accident. Write an article about the difficulty of the decisions made by both families and some of the problems that the families might encounter.

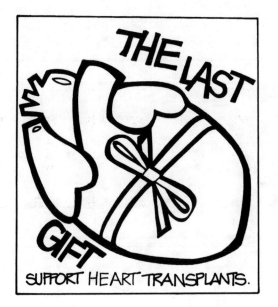

Extended Activities

1. Analyze the events in "A Brief History of Transplants" on page 56. Choose the two that, in your opinion, are most important to the advance of organ transplantation. In a short essay, explain why you chose those two. Then do more in-depth research on one of them, and write a summary of it. Include the following:

   > more information on the event
   > information on the doctor or researcher
   > why this particular event is considered a milestone
   > how the event may have influenced more research

2. After doing some research on organ transplantation, write a one-page report on another milestone that you think should be added to the "Brief History" of page 56. Explain why you chose that event.

3. Imagine that a person who is in jail for armed robbery has developed kidney failure and needs a transplant in order to survive. The following people have been called together to discuss the case and decide what should be done: the prisoner's physician, the prisoner's attorney, a surgeon who is a transplant specialist, a person willing to donate a healthy kidney to the patient, the victim of the patient's crime (wheelchair-bound as a result of being shot during the robbery), and you, who will act as mediator. Role-play the discussion with other students, or write a script in which these people share their opinions and expertise.

58

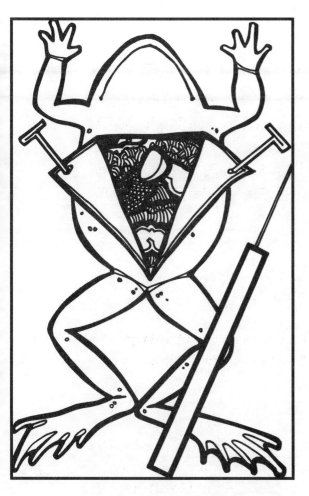

Animals & Science

What's the Issue?

Students dissect animals in the classroom, doctors use animals for medical experiments, and scientists in laboratories use animals to test medicines and other products such as cosmetics. Historically, the use of animals in experimentation dates back to the ancient Greeks and Romans, but a surge of opposition to the use of animals in the lab arose throughout Europe and the United States in the late 1800s.

The Society for the Protection of Animals Liable to Vivisection was founded in London in 1875 by Frances Power Cobbe. As a result of her campaigning, Britain became the first country to pass a law on the use of animals in the laboratory—the Cruelty to Animals Act of 1876.

In 1966, the United States Congress passed the Laboratory Animal Welfare Act. It was amended in 1970 and renamed the Animal Welfare Act and included the care of animals in research institutions. However, rats, mice, and birds, which account for about 85% of all laboratory animals, were excluded from the regulations.

The main issues in this controversy are whether or not animals should be used for classroom and medical experiments, and whether or not product safety testing should be done on animals.

THE ANIMAL WELFARE ACT

The Animal Welfare Act was signed into law in 1966. Its original intent was to regulate the care and use of animals in the laboratory, but it has become the only Federal law that regulates the treatment of animals in research, exhibition, transport, and by dealers. All other regulations refer to the Animal Welfare Act as the minimum acceptable standard.

The Regulations are divided into four sections. The first section describes exactly what is meant by certain terms in the legislation. The second section includes licensing, registration, research facilities, adequate veterinary care, stolen animals, compliance with standards, confiscation, and destruction of animals. The third section provides standards for specific species or groups of species including cats, dogs, guinea pigs, hamsters, rabbits, marine mammals, and other animals. The final section outlines the rules for administrative proceedings.

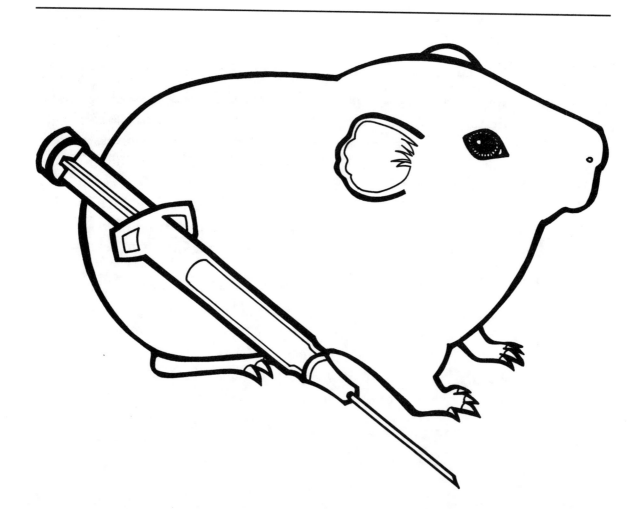

60

People opposed to animal experimentation argue that it is scientifically invalid. Because humans and other animals are so different, they say, the results obtained from research on animals cannot be applied to humans. They believe that animal experimentation is barbaric torture and amounts to cruelty to animals. Futhermore, opponents claim, many of the experiments performed on animals are pointless or repetitive of research that has already been done.

Animal behavorists have come to appreciate the tremendous complexity of animals' lives, including their ability to communicate, their range of emotions, and their responses to pain. This knowledge makes it nearly impossible to regard animals as mere laboratory supplies.

Opponents to the use of animals for experimentation argue that alternatives exist, such as magnetic resonance imaging, positron emission tomography, tissue culture, human studies, replacing vertebrates with simpler life forms such as worms, and computer modeling. New non-animal tests have proven to be more accurate than animal tests at predicting the safety of chemicals, according to opponents, and are also being used to design and test new drugs.

People in favor of animal experimentation argue that many major medical advances, including the use of insulin to treat diabetes, polio vaccines, antibiotics, organ transplantation, hip replacements, and drug treatments for ulcers, asthma, and high blood pressure, depended on animal experimentation. Human life expectancy has increased by 20.8 years because of discoveries made in research using animals, proponents say. For example, research into inherited childhood diseases like cystic fibrosis has made much progress because scientists can now reproduce in mice the same genetic defects that cause the diseases in humans. These animal models can be used to test new treatments quickly and easily. Doctors now predict the development of effective treatments for many inherited diseases in the next five to ten years.

By today's standards, the experiments of the past caused unacceptable levels of suffering in lab animals. Nowadays, and particularly over the past 30 years, stringent controls safeguard the welfare of laboratory animals, according to proponents of animal research.

Proponents also point out that the number of vertebrate animals used in research each year is less than 1 percent of the number killed for food, and that the majority of animals used in biomedical research are bred specifically for that purpose by USDA-licensed suppliers.

Furthermore, say proponents of animal research, new drugs are tested on humans as well. By the time they become available for prescription, most drugs have been tested on more humans than animals. Animal tests are designed to detect things like cancer, birth defects, organ failure, and the effects of acute poisoning. Once a drug is known to be safe enough it can start being tested on humans, where the most reliable information about side effects is discovered.

1. Find out whether a representative from the local Humane Society can be invited to talk to your class about animal rights and the purpose of the Humane Society. Prepare several thoughtful questions before the speaker arrives. Summarize the speaker's talk in a short essay, or share the information by making presentations to other classes. If a speaker cannot come to the classroom, perhaps the Humane Society could supply videos, posters, pamphlets, and addresses through which further information can be obtained.

2. Give a short talk to younger children on the humane care and treatment of animals. Outline the important points that you want to make. Use visual aids such as pictures, charts, and posters to make your talk more interesting. Discuss what physical, mental, or emotional needs of animals might go unmet in a research lab.

3. Put yourself in the position of a person who loves animals of all kinds, but also has a medical condition that is dependent on animal research in the search for a cure. Write a letter to the editor of your local newspaper explaining your situation and your opinion of animal research.

4. Debate whether or not animals should be used for testing shampoos and face creams. Use the "Tips for Discussions and Debates" on page 8.

5. As a biology teacher, you are required to give a lesson on dissecting frogs. You must decide whether or not to use preserved frogs from a biological supply company for your classroom lesson. Write a memo to your principal explaining your decision, the reasons for the decision, and a short description on how you will teach the lesson.

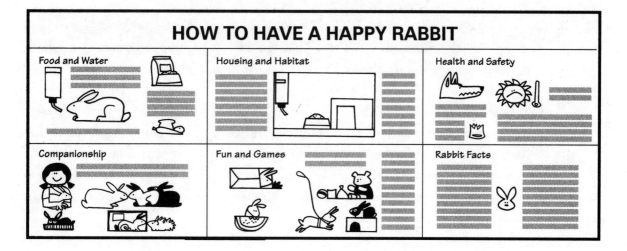

HOW TO HAVE A HAPPY RABBIT

Food and Water

Housing and Habitat

Health and Safety

Companionship

Fun and Games

Rabbit Facts

Extended Activities

1. Millions of animals are used in classrooms every year. Cats, frogs, fetal pigs, grasshoppers, earthworms, rats, mice, dogs, and pigeons are just some of the animals used. Most of the animals are purchased dead for dissection. Others are purchased live and vivisected (subjected to procedures while still alive). Still others are used in experiments for science fairs.

   Take a survey of students' opinions on animal dissection. Begin by writing several well-researched questions. Present the questions to ten students or more. Then write a short summary of the results of the survey. Do you agree with the results? Explain why or why not.

2. Learn more about the Animal Welfare Act by reading about it in reference books or finding info on the Animal Welfare Information Center Web site at http://www.nal.usda.gov/awic/.

   Share what you have learned by creating an informational brochure to help people better understand the act. Then, in a short paragraph, create one rule or regulation that you think would make the Animal Welfare Act better.

3. There are some alternatives to using animals for experiments, for example, magnetic resonance imaging, tissue culture, and computer modeling. Pretend that you are a scientist in the twenty-second century. You are world famous for your imaginative inventions, especially one that is the perfect alternative to one form of animal experimentation. Describe your fantastic invention, draw a picture of it, and label its components.

TOPIC #8

Genetically Modified Food

What's the Issue?

Humans have been experimenting with their crops for over 10,000 years, trying to make plants that are ideally suited to their needs. Techniques such as selective breeding (saving seeds from the best plants for replanting) and cross-breeding (combining traits from different species to give plants more desirable qualities) have been successful, but are imprecise and unpredictable. It wasn't until the discovery of DNA in the 1950s and the development of techniques to modify DNA, that scientists had the ability to breed crops using an entirely new technique—genetic engineering.

Genes are the blueprints of living organisms, and genetic engineering is the process of artificially altering those blueprints by inserting genes to give organisms new traits. For example, plants such as corn, potatoes, and soybeans are genetically modified to resist insect infestation and to withstand herbicides used to kill weeds. Other foods that are already genetically modified, or are very likely to be in the near future, include apples, lentils, lettuce, peas, pineapple, tomatoes, and wheat.

Genetic engineering might seem like a futuristic concept, but Americans have been eating genetically modified crops for more than five years. However, the appearance of genetically modified foods in the marketplace has resulted in a surge of public debate and scientific discussion. The issue that most concerns consumers, environmentalists, and scientists is whether or not genetically modified foods are safe for humans and/or farm animals to eat, and safe for the environment. Another issue being debated is whether or not genetically modified foods should be identified by mandatory labeling.

TACO SHELL RECALL

StarLink is the name of a genetically modified variety of corn approved for animal use, but not approved for human use for fear it will trigger allergic reactions. When tests by an environmental group were conducted, it was found that StarLink corn had illegally entered supplies intended for human consumption and was found in, among other products, taco shells. The incident raises serious questions about whether genetically engineered products can be kept segregated from conventional ones in the nation's food system.

StarLink commented that the corn was apparently sold by farmers to dozens or even hundreds of grain elevators across the country, which unknowingly distributed it to millers and processors for use in making food. Many makers of tortillas and taco shells voluntarily withdrew some of their products. Some grocery stores did the same.

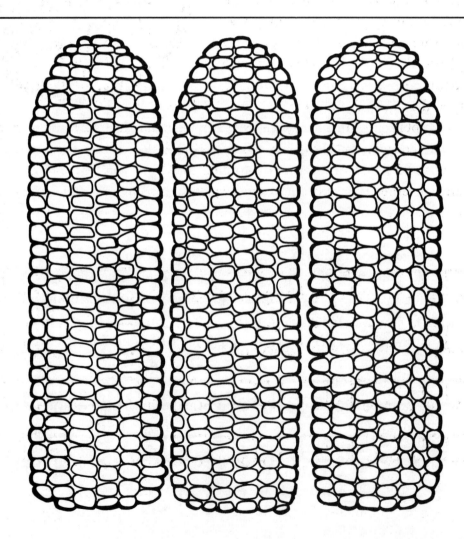

One of the main concerns of supporters of genetic engineering is world hunger. They maintain that the increased yield of genetically modified food crops would make hunger a thing of the past.

Proponents also point out that genetic engineering allows scientists to create foods with extra nutrients. For example, the biotechnology industry has been promoting "golden rice," modified to contain extra vitamin A, which they claim will help cure vitamin A deficiency, which can lead to night blindness in malnourished people. In addition, the future may bring bread that can help lower cholesterol or engineered vegetables packed with cancer-fighting ingredients, according to proponents.

Many people involved in growing crops support genetic modification. Some genetically modified crops can fight off bugs without the use of chemical pesticides, so genetically engineered foods could be less harsh on the environment. Modifications to plants can help protect them against some changes in climate, as well as produce plants that are productive in harsh growing conditions like extreme heat, drought, soil salinity, and other climatic stresses.

Orthodox rabbis and Muslim leaders have ruled that simple modifications that lead to one or a few new components in a species are acceptable for kosher foods prepared according to Jewish law and halal foods prepared according to Islamic law. Some religious leaders, however, are concerned that genetically modified food might contain genes from animals such as swine that are prohibited by some religions.

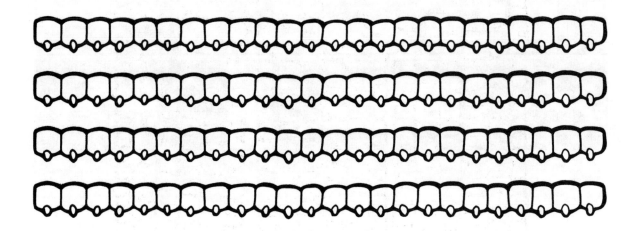

Proponents argue that genetic engineering results in food that is as safe for humans, animals, and the environment as food produced by conventional technologies, but people opposed to genetically engineered foods say that that is not necessarily true. Genetically engineered plants could prove allergenic or otherwise harmful to humans, they say. For example, if new genes inadvertently cause a plant to produce toxins at higher levels than are present naturally, there could be long-term health consequences for humans.

Opponents worry that genetic engineering poses ecological risks, too. For example, one experiment demonstrated that it was possible to create new strains of weeds resistant to herbicides. Such super-weeds could severely decrease crop productivity. Genetically modified plants could alter the ecology of natural plant communities and disrupt natural food chains. Who would be liable if traditional crops or fields were ruined because of cross-pollination with genetically modified plants?

Opponents are also concerned that genetic engineering will lead to increased control of agriculture by biotechnology corporations. For example, farmers who plant patented, modified corn are forbidden to take seed from their harvest for the next year's planting, but must buy new seed. Opponents fear that such restrictions will result in world food production being dominated by a few companies.

Especially important to people who are opposed to genetic engineering is the issue of labeling modified foods to give consumers a choice whether or not they want to purchase those foods. Currently, there is no requirement in the United States that genetically engineered foods be labeled as such, but many other countries, including Great Britain, France, Germany, the Netherlands, Belgium, Luxembourg, Denmark, Sweden, Finland, Ireland, Spain, Austria, Italy, Portugal, Greece, New Zealand, and Japan do have labeling requirements for genetically altered foods.

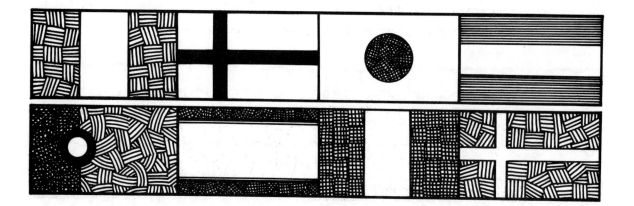

68

1. The president of a canned corn company wants to create a special label for the genetically engineered corn that the company produces. You have been hired for the job. Think about what information should be required on a label for genetically engineered foods. Make a list of the important points. Then draw the label.

2. Pretend you are a scientist who has the ability to modify any plant. Use your imagination to modify a plant in either a practical or fanciful way. Draw pictures of both the old plant and the modified plant. Label the changes that were made, and explain why you made them.

3. Create a regulatory agency to oversee the production of your modified plant. Make a brochure or pamphlet that explains the various components of your agency's regulatory system. Include information that answers the following questions:

   Will the agency you create be part of an already existing government agency, or will you need to create a new agency?

   What expertise will members of the agency possess?

   What kinds of testing will you conduct to make sure your modified plant is safe?

   Will the agency be able to reject unsafe products?

   How will the agency educate the public about its purpose and standards?

4. Debate the topic of whether or not genetically modified foods should be labeled as such. (Use the "Tips for Discussions and Debates" on page 8.)

1. Analyze the "Taco Shell Recall" story on page 66. If you were to interview each of the people listed below, what do you think their responses to the story would be? Write short paragraphs summarizing the response of each person.

   the president of StarLink

   a director of the Aztec Tortilla Company

   a manager of ShopAway grocery store

   an owner of the Taco Loco restaurant

   a representative from the United States Department of Agriculture

   a teenager who loves tacos

   a representative from Protect Our Plants, an environmental group

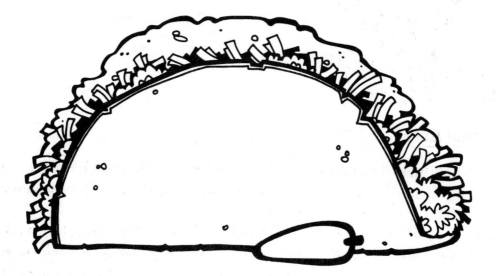

70

Relocating Wolves

What's the Issue?

What do you think of when you hear the word "wolf?" Children often have stereotypes (fixed ideas) about wolves from reading "Little Red Riding Hood," "The Three Little Pigs," Aesop's fables, and other fairytales and myths.

Humans have had a long and complex relationship with wolves. Many Native American cultures revered the wolf which played a prominent role in their cultures and spiritual beliefs. Early fur traders were indifferent to the presence of wolves because the wolves posed no threat. Negative attitudes toward wolves were common among early settlers in the American West because wolves were a menace to their livestock. As settlers encroached further and further into wolves' territory, wolves began to prey on settlers' livestock. In response, many states and regions put a bounty on wolves offering to pay hunters and trappers who turned in dead wolves. The wolf population started to decline, and by the late 1920s, wolves were either extinct or rare in all of the United States.

In 1973, Congress passed the Endangered Species Act, and, in the following years, wolf recovery programs were started to reintroduce the wolf to its natural habitat. Today, ranchers, environmentalists, home owners, and government officials are involved in ongoing disputes over whether and where wolves should be allowed to roam. Creating a plan to reintroduce wolves in certain areas has proven difficult and has faced great opposition. The plan requires a balancing act among ranchers and conservationists, and there are extremists on both sides.

IMPORTANT EVENTS THAT LED TO THE REINTRODUCTION OF THE WOLF TO YELLOWSTONE NATIONAL PARK

1872 Congress sets aside Yellowstone as the first National Park.

1916 The National Park Service is established to protect and conserve the nation's parks.

1935 Governmental wolf bounties come to an end in order to comply with a newly established National Park Service policy.

1962 An environmental awakening comes with the publication of Rachel Carson's *Silent Spring*. Carson would provide the impetus for a series of strict environmental laws, including the Rare and Endangered Species Act (1966) and the Endangered Species Act (1973).

1973 The Fish and Wildlife Service lists the Rocky Mountain gray wolf as an endangered species. The Endangered Species Act mandates that the government attempt by all means possible to recover the populations of species listed as endangered. For the wolf, this means reintroduction.

72

People opposed to wolf restoration argue that the wolf is not actually in danger of becoming extinct. There are thousands of wolves in Canada and Alaska, and more than 2000 in Minnesota, Wisconsin, and Michigan.

That wolves kill livestock and pets is the chief complaint of ranchers and farmers. They are concerned that wolves released by the government will kill their livestock and even drive them out of business. There is no fence to prevent the wolves introduced into Yellowstone National Park from moving outside the park onto private lands where livestock may be present. Ranchers maintain that the government acted against the law in establishing the wolf restoration program, in that the government put wolves in the middle of their ranch land but did not allow the ranchers the means to protect their livestock.

People in favor of wolf restoration argue that the wolf controls the populations of other wild animals. Wolves generally prey upon the weak, the old, and the young. When wolves are removed from an area, the big game animals suffer major bouts of starvation and disease. Advocates of wolf restoration point out that although wolves may attack livestock or pets, section 10(j) of the Endangered Species Act does permit a wolf to be killed if caught in the act of killing livestock on private land. Also, wildlife agents can trap and remove the offending animal.

While wolves pose some threat to domestic animals, there is little risk to people themselves, say their advocates. Whereas humans have killed an estimated two million wolves in this century, there is not a single documented case of a human being killed by a healthy wild wolf. Neither the livestock industry nor the economy of the areas in which wolves are reintroduced are affected by wolf predation, according to proponents of restoration. Advocates also point out that the government compensates ranchers for lost sheep and cattle.

1. Pretend that the American Wolf Association has assigned you the job of creating a good image for the wolf. They would like you to do one, or all, of the following tasks:

   Rewrite "The Three Little Pigs" or "Little Red Riding Hood" so that the wolf is the hero of the story.

   Create a new type of werewolf legend that depicts a werewolf as a comic book-type of superhero along the lines of Superman and Batman.

   Create a poster showing a family of wolves in their natural habitat.

2. Learn more about the gray wolf through research in your public or school library or on the Internet. Two sites that have lots of well-documented information are the University of Michigan's Animal Diversity Web stie at http://animaldiversity.ummz.umich.edu (do a search for "wolf" and click on "*Canis lupus lycaon*") and "Nova: Wild Wolves" at http://www.pbs.org/wgbh/nova/wolves/.

3. Create an educational brochure using the information you found in your research. Include pictures, maps, and text. Also include a personal opinion section in which you state your opinion on whether or not wolves should be reintroduced into national parks. Share the brochure with younger children, or give a copy to your school library.

4. Write a story or poem based on the following incident:

   A rancher has cattle grazing on his land, which is near a wolf reintroduction area. One morning he finds the mangled carcass of a calf. Ranchers, rangers, and environmental specialists meet to discuss the incident. Tempers flare.

5. Debate the proposition: "Wolves should not be reintroduced into Yellowstone Park." Use the "Tips for Discussions and Debates" on page 8.

QUOTES FROM JOHN MUIR

"When we try to pick out anything by itself, we find it hitched to everything else in the universe."

"When one tugs at a single thing in nature, he finds it attached to the rest of the world."

"Brought into right relationships with the wilderness, man would see that his appropriation of Earth's resources beyond his personal needs would only bring imbalance and beget ultimate loss and poverty by all."

Extended Activities

1. John Muir (1839–1914) was a botanist who had a passion for adventure, discovery, and travel. He helped found the first environmental organization in North America, the Sierra Club, and served as its first president. Read the "Quotes from John Muir," on page 75. As you read the quotes think about how they might relate to the topic of wolf restoration. Choose one of the quotes to interpret in a collage, poem, or creative writing on wolves. Use Muir's quote somewhere in your work.

2. If you were a naturalist like Muir, what would be your opinion of the following topics?

> Putting a bounty on wolves
> Reintroducing wolves into Yellowstone National Park
> The concern of ranchers about the predatory nature of wolves

3. Research wolves as characters in books. Read one of the books you found out about, or one of the suggested books below. Write a book review in which you comment on the image of wolves in the book, the way the human characters interacted with the wolves, and the author's attitude toward wolves. (Possible books are *Julie's Wolf Pack*, *Julie of the Wolves*, and *Nutik the Wolf Pup*, all by Jean Craighead George; and *Wolves of Willoughby Chase* by Joan Aiken.)

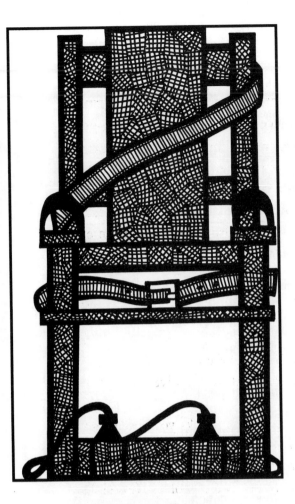

Capital Punishment

What's the Issue?

In some countries, criminals who commit certain crimes can be put to death for those crimes. This method of punishment is called capital punishment. Usually capital punishment is imposed for murder, but it has also been used for other crimes, including robbery, kidnapping, and treason. According to Amnesty International, in the year 2000, nearly 1,500 prisoners were executed in 27 countries, including 85 in the United States.

Governments of countries and states prescribe various methods of execution. Those used in the United States include hanging, firing squad, electrocution, gas chamber, and lethal injection. Twelve states (Alaska, Hawaii, Iowa, Maine, Massachusetts, Michigan, Minnesota, North Dakota, Rhode Island, Vermont, West Virginia, and Wisconsin) and the District of Columbia do not have the death penalty.

The most important issues surrounding capital punishment are whether or not the execution of criminals is ever justified, and, if so, under what circumstances. Complicating these issues are questions about whether or not insane persons should be put to death, whether disparities between races occur, and whether or not juvenile offenders should be executed.

No issue of capital punishment disturbs people on both sides of the issue more than the possibility that an innocent person might be executed. Our judicial system is intended to protect the innocent, but it is not foolproof. In January 2000, Governor George H. Ryan of Illinois declared a moratorium on executions because thirteen people on death row were found to have been wrongfully convicted. Other states, too, are examining their criminal justice system in light of the large number of people who were sentenced to death and later were able to prove their innocence by access to new evidence or DNA tests that were not available at the original trials.

EARLY HISTORY OF CAPITAL PUNISHMENT LAWS

c. 1700 B.C. The Code of King Hammurabi of Babylon prescribes the death penalty for 25 different crimes.

c. 1300 B.C. The death penalty is a part of the Hittite Code.

c. 600 B.C. The death penalty is punishment for all crimes in the Code of Athens.

c. 450 B.C. The Roman Law of Twelve Tablets sanctions the death penalty.

C. A.D. 1056 William the Conqueror outlaws the death penalty in England, except in times of war. This prohibition would last until the 16th century.

A.D. 1608 Captain George Kendall is convicted of spying for Spain and executed at Jamestown, Virginia—the first recorded execution in the American colonies.

1700s In Britain, 222 crimes are punishable by death, including stealing, cutting down a tree, and robbing a rabbit warren.

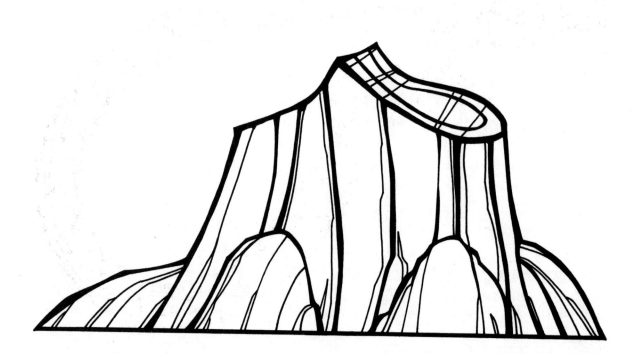

People who favor capital punishment feel that it is justified because it obviously prevents criminals from repeating their crimes, and it acts as a deterrent to crime by discouraging would-be offenders. Critics of capital punishment wonder if the same things could be accomplished by less severe punishment, for example long-term or life imprisonment. Critics believe that life imprisonment can be an even more powerful deterrent than capital punishment.

Some advocates of capital punishment feel that retribution is sometimes justified or even required. For example, if someone murders a person, then the murderer must be killed, too. Sometimes this is called taking "an eye for an eye." However, critics point out that retribution cannot be applied uniformly to every crime committed. For example, if a terrorist kills ten people, the taking the terrorist's life is technically not sufficient retribution. Critics also argue that retribution is really just vengeance, which shouldn't be part of a decision on life or death.

Some supporters of capital punishment argue that when a person commits a crime, he or she forfeits all rights, and society may punish the criminal in any way it sees fit. An opposing viewpoint is that criminals must forfeit some of their rights, like freedom to travel, hold certain jobs, or vote; but they do not necessarily forfeit the right to life.

Opponents of capital punishment contend that it should be abolished because it is undignified and inhumane. After all, they say, flogging and burning at the stake are no longer accepted practices, and capital punishment should be abolished too. They also argue that capital punishment violates the Eighth Amendment to the U.S. Constitution, which states that "excessive bail shall not be required, nor excessive fines imposed, *nor cruel and unusual punishments inflicted*."

Defenders of capital punishment say that the "cruel and unusual punishment" argument has no historical basis. When the Constitution was drafted, capital punishment was practiced widely, and not considered cruel or unusual. In fact, many framers of the Constitution endorsed capital punishment.

There is some disagreement as to whether death sentences are applied fairly. Studies show that people on death row are typically poor and cannot afford the best defense trial. They are also predominately black and Hispanic, which raises the issue of racial equality.

80

1. After studying the issues surrounding capital punishment, write a letter to a judge explaining why you would or would not be able to serve as a juror on a capital case. The judge will need to see that you have carefully thought through the issues, so state the reasons for your decision.

2. Hold a debate on one of these capital punishment propositions (use the "Tips for Discussions and Debates" on page 8):

   "Capital punishment is justified for all murder cases."

   "Capital punishment is appropriate for juveniles for certain offenses."

   "Life imprisonment is harsher than capital punishment for most major offenses, including murder."

3. Make a list of deterrents to bad behavior in the following places: at school, at home, in your neighborhood, in the mall.

4. Does your state allow capital punishment? Talk to public officials, or use other resource materials, to find answers to these questions. Summarize your findings in a short essay.

   What is the history of your state's policy on using or prohibiting capital punishment?

   Has your state ever had a different policy on capital punishment? Explain.

   Are the majority of your state's residents happy with the current policy?

   If your state has capital punishment, does it seem to work as a deterrent to crime?

6. Make a list of five crimes that you consider very serious, and rank them in order of severity. Put a star by each crime you think deserves the death penalty. Explain your decisions in a paragraph following your list.

Extended Activities

1. Read the information in the chart "Early History of Capital Punishment Laws." Choose one of the time periods represented there (ancient Mesopotamia, the Hittite empire, ancient Greece, ancient Rome, medieval England, or colonial America) and use reference books and the Internet to find out about the laws that governed the people of that period, and how the laws were enforced. Summarize your findings in the form of an oral report, a chart, or an informational brochure.

2. Find out about the forms of governments and legal systems of other countries that permit capital punishment. Compare and contrast the governments and legal systems of one or two of these countries with the government and legal system of the United States.

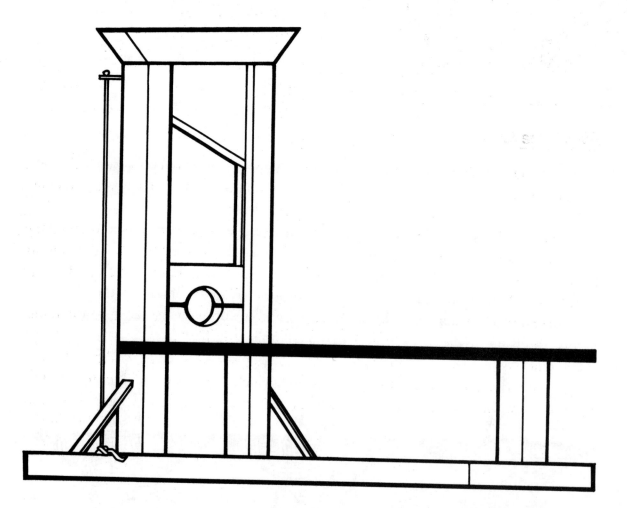

Immigration

What's the Issue?

Since the 1600s, millions of people have left their homelands to live in America. They have come from all corners of the world to escape economic hardship, to find religious and political freedom, and to try their fortunes in a new land.

There has always been intense national debate on the subject of immigration, and there still is. There are two categories of immigration, legal and illegal. Each year, the U.S. admits between 700,000 and 900,000 legal immigrants. In addition, about 275,000 people enter the country illegally each year.

Government officials agree that illegal immigration is a serious problem. Legal immigration, however, is another matter. Experts are sharply divided over whether the U.S.'s immigration policy should open the borders to all people, or restrict either the number of people allowed to immigrate or the countries from which they may come. This has become an even more controversial topic since the September 11, 2001, terrorist attacks on our country.

Copyright © 2003 The Learning Works

IMMIGRATION RESTRICTION LEAGUE

The Immigration Restriction League (IRL) was founded in Boston in 1894 by people who wanted to limit the rising numbers of immigrants coming to the United States.

Traditionally, the United States had an open-door policy toward immigrants. After the 1870s, many people from southern and eastern Europe immigrated. Some Americans were prejudiced toward the darker skinned people. The IRL sought to restrict immigration by raising literacy requirements. Since many of the new immigrants did not know how to read, a literacy requirement would be an effective barrier to their admission to the country.

The IRL gained support and influence, persuading Congress to pass literacy bills. The first, in 1897, was vetoed by President Grover Cleveland. The second, passed in 1917, passed on a wave of anti-immigrant hysteria resulting from World War I and the Russian Revolution.

The IRL eventually dissolved, but not before influencing the passing of the Quota Act of 1924, which restricted immigration according to the national origins of the immigrants except those coming from Canada, Newfoundland, Mexico, Cuba, Haiti, the Dominican Republic, the Canal Zone, and the independent countries of Central and South America.

Sensible immigration is a good thing: It invigorates our society and makes life more interesting for us all. This is one of the main arguments of people who support open immigration. The same people also point out that the United States is one of the richest countries in the world, and argue that it should allow the poor, the sick, the suffering, and those who are seeking something bigger and better into our country. We have the space, the economy, and the resources to help them, and immigration advocates believe that it is in everyone's interest that we do so.

Advocates also suggest that employers can keep labor costs low by hiring immigrants, who are willing to work for less pay than Americans. Advocates say that most immigrants become hard-working taxpayers, eager to learn English and to be seen as Americans.

The cost of open immigration concerns many who propose limiting the number of people who enter the United States. They say that the claim that immigrants pay more in taxes than they receive in services is misleading, pointing out that services like roads, hospitals, and police and fire protection are not included in most statistical studies, and that many immigrants work for cash only and do not pay taxes. Immigrants, say their detractors, are more likely to become dependent on public assistance than those who are native-born.

In the opinion of those who would restrict immigration, immigrants who do not learn English or assimilate in other ways destroy the shared cultural identity of Americans. Some also claim that most immigrants who come here under family-reunification laws do so for economic reasons, not because they miss their families.

Some minority communities worry that annual quotas of immigration are too high and should be reduced; they feel that immigrants create too much competition for low-skilled jobs, edging out native-born Americans.

Activities

1. Find out more about the people who are immigrating to the United States in the 21st century. Do research to discover where they are coming from and why they are leaving their own countries. Use the resources in libraries and on the Internet to research this topic. Then make a chart, graph, or map to summarize your findings.

2. What is life like for immigrants coming to the U.S. today? Talk to representatives from federal, state, or community immigration organizations, or invite a recent immigrant to talk to your class. Based on what you have learned, write a short story, poem, or essay that describes what it is like to be an immigrant.

3. If you were the director in charge of immigration into America, what would be your guiding principles in deciding what quotas to set and whom to admit or refuse? Express your philosophy in a letter to the president of the United States. Also, tell the president why you think we do or do not need immigration reform.

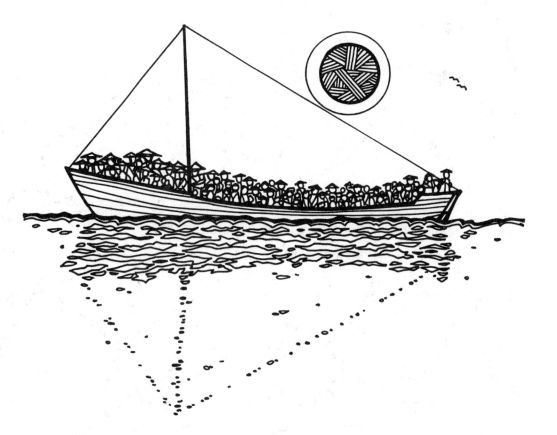

86

4. Imagine that you are an immigrant who entered the United States at Ellis Island in 1905. Write a diary in which you tell about your journey, where you came from, your arrival at the island, and how you are adapting to life in America. There are numerous sites on the Internet to help in your research. One interesting site is "Explore Your Family History at Ellis Island" at www.ellisisland.org/Immexp/index.asp?.

5. Choose three countries and evaluate the current status of immigration in each. Compare each country's immigration policies to those of the United States. In what ways are they similar? In what ways do they differ? (Consider researching some of these countries: Germany, Israel, Canada, Australia, India, Japan, Egypt.) Write a detailed report giving your findings.

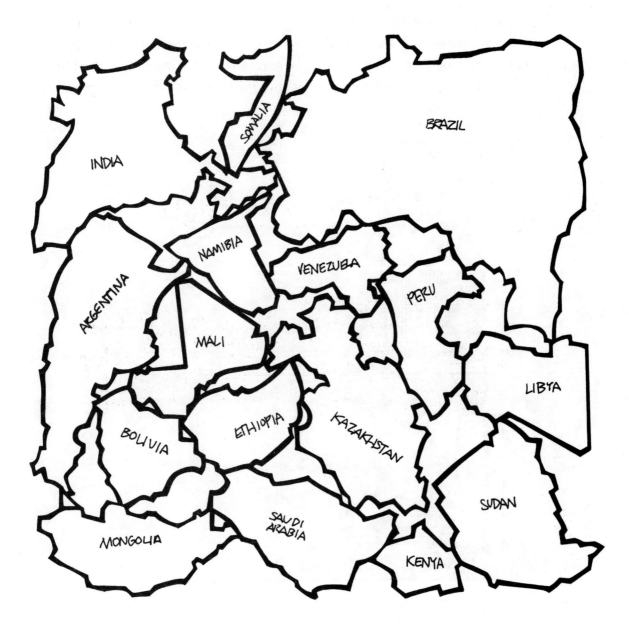

Extended Activities

1. Read the profile of the Immigration Restriction League on page 84. Would you have been a supporter of the Immigration Restriction League in 1894? What were the concerns of the people living in Boston at that time? Why do you think they formed the IRL? Pretend that you are the editor of a Boston newspaper in the 1890s. Write an editorial expressing your view of the league, and of immigration in general.

2. Research one of the following:

   Quota Act of 1924
   Chinese Exclusion Act (1882)
   Gentleman's Agreement (1906)
   Dillingham Commission (1907)

   In the role of a U.S. senator of the appropriate period, make an argument that might have been made in Congress expressing your support or opposition. Present your argument in an oral presentation or a written speech.

88

Terrorism & Civil Rights

What's the Issue?

Shortly after the September 11, 2001, terrorist attacks on the World Trade Center in New York City and the Pentagon in Washington, D.C., the United States Congress passed several bills to help prevent future terrorist attacks. One of these, called the USA Patriot Act, granted the government extensive powers to investigate, observe, and wiretap terrorist suspects; greater power to investigate records of e-mails and Internet use; and the power to detain non-citizens without bringing specific charges. Governments often react to emergencies by reducing certain civil liberties such as freedom of speech, movement, and assembly.

The September 11 crisis, with its shocking violence, has led to many emergency arrangements and new laws that some people claim restrict civil rights unacceptably. Most people hope that these new laws and regulations will protect people from future terrorist attacks. But they have also raised several questions. If terrorist attacks continue, will law enforcement and intelligence agencies need even more power? Do the new laws and regulations infringe on the civil rights of United States citizens and non-citizens?

People who are concerned about both national security and civil rights want laws that balance the need for effective protections against the right of innocent Americans and innocent non-citizens to be free from government surveillance. They are concerned that the USA Patriot Act circumvents the checks and balances that traditionally protect individual liberty.

The most troubling provisions of the USA Patriot Act, they argue, are measures that allow for indefinite detention of non-citizens because of minor visa violations, expanded power for telephone and Internet surveillance by law enforcement, increased power for the government to conduct searches, and for the FBI to have access to sensitive business records about individuals without having to show evidence of a crime. They also worry about the possibility of broad investigations of American citizens for "intelligence" purposes.

People who support the broad new security measures point out that the terrorist attacks of September 11 call for extreme measures to protect the people of the United States. They argue that the Constitution permits a distinction between citizens and non-citizens, especially in matters of national security. Citizens benefit from equal protection privileges, due process clauses, and individual liberties like speech. But according to Supreme Court rulings, non-citizens are entitled only to some of those privileges and protections. For example, during times of a terrorist threat, both Congress and the president have the power to exclude non-citizens from the country and to scrutinize the behavior of non-citizens in ways that the Constitution would not permit with regard to American citizens.

90

Those concerned about civil rights for both citizens and non-citizens argue that although non-citizens do not enjoy all of the rights accorded to citizens—for example, the right to vote—the Supreme Court has found that non-citizens still have fundamental human rights that cannot be violated.

Most people on both sides of the issue want to prevent the persecution of citizens and non-citizens that has occurred throughout American history during times of national upheaval and crisis. One example of such persecution is the detainment of Japanese-Americans during World War II. Under Executive Order 9066, signed by President Franklin Roosevelt on February 19, 1942, all Japanese and Americans of Japanese ancestry were removed from western coastal regions to guarded camps in the interior. Some people fear that a similar policy will be adopted now or in the future.

Activities

1. Participate in a class discussion of what personal liberties you are willing to sacrifice to protect yourself from future terrorist attacks. In your opinion, what elements of American democracy are too important to give up? What are some possible security risks facing Americans when they live by the freedoms granted in the Bill of Rights?

2. Do some research to identify times in United States history when the government curtailed civil liberties. Some examples are the Civil War when Lincoln suspended the writ of *habeas corpus*; World War I and the Espionage Act; 1796 and the Alien and Sedition Act; World War II and the Japanese internment camps; and the Cold War and the treatment of suspected Communists. Make a chart with columns for the event, year, people involved, liberties curtailed, and outcome, and list at least three such events.

3. How much protection, if any, do you think non-citizens should be given under the Bill of Rights while they are living in the United States? Write a letter to the editor of your local newspaper expressing your opinion.

4. For each of the following circumstances, write a short paragraph explaining what you think should be done.

   A college student is held by the FBI after an interview reveals that she has relatives who are connected with the Afghan Taliban.
   A visitor from Asia is caught traveling within the United States with an expired visa.
   A resident non-citizen from Brazil is overheard criticizing United States policy in South America.

5. Debate this proposition: "Sometimes it is necessary to curtail certain civil liberties, and after terrorist attacks is one of those times." (Use the "Tips for Discussions and Debates" on page 8)

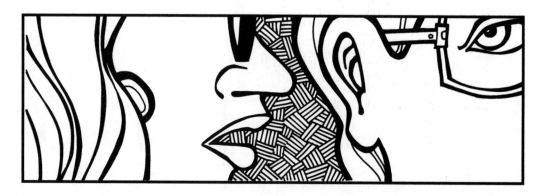

1. When unpopular laws are enacted, there is often open resistance to them. Resistance is demonstrated in many different ways—by letters to officials, newspapers, or magazines; television ads; political cartoons; protest marches; hunger strikes; mob violence; and even war. Write an essay explaining why you would or would not protest the loss of civil rights, and how you would express your feelings.

2. Do research to learn about occasions on which Americans have used non-violent demonstrations, sit-ins, and hunger strikes to protest a law or public policy. Make an oral report to your class about one of these occasions explaining the political situation, the type of protest used, and whether or not the protest was successful.

3. The internment of Japanese-Americans during World War II reminds us that we should not assume that our rights will always be secure. Learn more about Executive Order No. 9066, and *Korematsu v. United States*. Then answer these questions, either by discussing them with classmates or by writing a short response to each:

   Do you think that something similar to the Japanese-American internment could happen again?

   Why do you think Japanese-Americans were interned while citizens of Italian and German descent were not?

   Do you approve of or disapprove of the letter that President Bill Clinton wrote apologizing to Japanese-Americans? Why, or why not?

The White House
Washington
October 1, 1993

Over fifty years ago, the United States Government unjustly interned, evacuated, or relocated you and many other Japanese Americans. Today, on behalf of your fellow Americans, I offer a sincere apology to you for the actions that unfairly denied Japanese Americans and their families fundamental liberties during World War II.

In passing the Civil Liberties Act of 1988, we acknowledged the wrongs of the past and offered redress to those who endured such grave injustice. In retrospect, we understand that the nation's actions were rooted deeply in racial prejudice, wartime hysteria, and a lack of political leadership. We must learn from the past and dedicate ourselves as a nation to renewing the spirit of equality and our love of freedom. Together, we can guarantee a future with liberty and justice for all. You and your family have my best wishes for the future.

[signed]
Bill Clinton

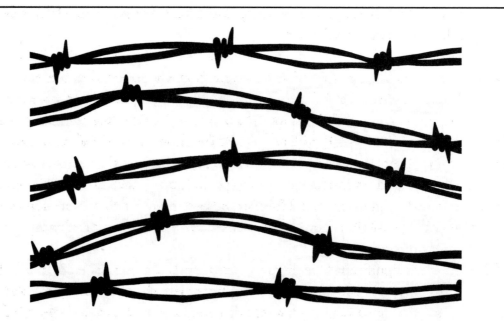

94

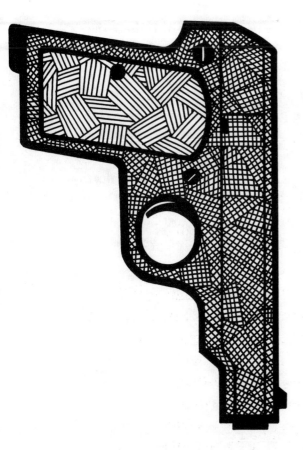

Gun Control

What's the Issue?

Gun control is a sensitive issue that evokes strong emotions in people on both sides. The long-running debate on how to curb gun violence in America gained momentum after the April 20, 1999, shooting at Columbine High School in Littleton, Colorado, in which two teenage gunmen killed 15 people. Historically, the debate over gun control has intensified following such prominent acts of violence.

Until 1934, there were no gun laws. It was legal to own and carry a gun at all times and in all places. In that year, however, the first gun legislation was passed after someone tried to assassinate President Franklin D. Roosevelt. The law forbade the sale of sawed-off shotguns, machine guns, and automatic weapons, and imposed a $200 fine for their possession.

After the assassinations of President John F. Kennedy, presidential candidate Robert Kennedy, and civil rights leader Martin Luther King, Jr., the Gun Control Act of 1968 was passed. This act imposed safety standards on imported guns, which raised their prices, and banned the purchase of guns by mail. However, because no restrictions were placed on domestic products, the legislation allowed U.S. arms manufacturers to market cheap handguns without foreign competition.

The most recent significant federal gun control legislation was passed in 1993, after an assassination attempt on President Ronald Reagan that left Press Secretary Jim Brady paralyzed. The Brady Act imposed a five-day waiting period and a background check before the purchase of a handgun. While more than 250,000 people have been denied the right to purchase a gun because of these restrictions, guns sold at gun shows and flea markets are exempted by the law, and require no background checks or waiting periods.

The United States is one of the most heavily armed countries in the developed world, with a homicide rate higher than that of any other developed country. This is a concern to many people, especially as it relates to child safety. The Centers for Disease Control and Prevention reported that in 1997, 4,223 Americans ages 19 and younger were killed or killed themselves with guns. Accidental shooting deaths are the second leading cause of death among children and teenagers. Despite the fact that there are now more than 20,000 gun laws on record in the U.S., the problem of gun violence has not ended. Most people agree that it is time for everyone to work together to stop gun violence. The controversy is over how to do that.

THE SECOND AMENDMENT

A well-regulated Militia being necessary to the security of a free State, the right of the people to keep and bear arms shall not be infringed.

Focus on the Controversy

Some people believe that the Second Amendment to the United States Constitution says that all citizens have the right to own guns. The National Rifle Association (NRA), a powerful lobbying group, believes that the right to keep and bear arms is a constitutional safeguard as worthy of defense as freedom of speech, assembly, and the press. On the other hand, proponents of gun control warn that the first part of the amendment—"a well-regulated Militia being necessary to the security of a free State"—defeats this argument. They point out that when the U.S. Constitution was adopted, each of the states had its own "militia," a military force composed of ordinary citizens serving as part-time soldiers. It was a well-regulated force intended to protect the new nation from outside forces and from internal rebellions.

The U.S. Supreme Court ruled in *U.S. v. Miller* (1939) that the "obvious purpose" of the Second Amendment was to "assure the continuation and render possible the effectiveness" of state militias. The Supreme Court addressed the Second Amendment twice more, upholding New Jersey's strict gun control law in 1969 and upholding a federal law banning felons from possessing guns in 1980.

Another area of special concern in the gun-control controversy is child safety. Many people argue that mandatory child safety locks on guns would help. Some gun manufacturers, like Smith & Wesson, have volunteered to add safety locks to their guns. Smith & Wesson has also proposed to make it impossible for anyone but the gun's owner to fire the weapon. However, the NRA criticized these steps as attacks on law-abiding gun owners, and many NRA members have refused to buy Smith & Wesson guns because they say that such restrictions infringe on their constitutional rights.

Many people feel that in order to own or use a gun, an individual should complete a gun education course similar to a driver training course. Many people also agree that guns should be licensed. They argue that if we can license and register cars, we should be able to license and register guns.

Some groups advocate raising the legal minimum age for gun ownership from 18 to 21, and requiring tougher background checks and longer waiting periods before guns can be purchased. People opposed to gun control say that such measures would reduce weapon sales—especially at gun shows, as the waiting periods would outlast the gun shows. According to the NRA, numerous studies on the effects of waiting periods, both before and after the Brady Bill was passed, have shown no correlation between waiting periods and murder or robbery rates. It is the NRA's opinion that waiting periods have no significant effect.

There is also a growing consensus that passing new laws is not the answer to gun violence. Some cities, for example, have turned from legislation to litigation, choosing to sue gun manufacturers in court rather than wait for laws to be passed. Their goal is to retrieve some of the $4 billion spent each year because of gun violence.

Proponents of gun control point out that lower murder rates in foreign countries prove that gun control works. In 1996, for example, handguns were used to murder 15 people in Japan, 30 in Britain, 106 in Canada—and 9,390 in the United States. A rebuttal submitted by the NRA points out that in Israel and Switzerland, a license to possess guns is available on demand to every law-abiding adult, and that both countries also allow widespread carrying of concealed firearms. Yet Switzerland and Israel have low rates of homicide.

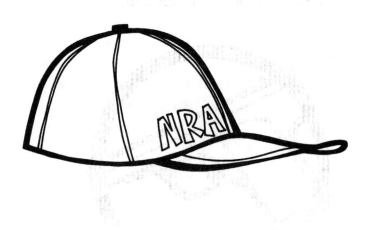

1. The editor of a newspaper has assigned you to write an article about gun-control laws and how they affect young people in your community. Interview key people in the debate, include graphs and/or tables, and quote prominent people in the gun control controversy.

2. Draw a political cartoon illustrating your position on gun control.

3. Research gun control laws and gun violence in Canada, Mexico, Great Britain, Israel, or Germany. Make a chart comparing statistics on gun use and gun violence in both the U.S. and the country you researched.

4. Pretend that you have been invited by your school to attend a conference on gun control. The keynote speech is entitled "Why We Need New and Stricter Gun Laws." When the speech is over, interview a representative from each of the groups below and write down three or four sentences highlighting their thoughts on the speech.

    A National Rifle Association member
    A gun show dealer
    A FBI agent
    A witness to a school shooting
    A legislator
    A hunter
    A Smith & Wesson representative

1. How do you interpret the Second Amendment? Does it grant a universal right to gun ownership, or is it limited to militias? Write your opinions and thoughts in a letter to a friend in Canada who doesn't understand the controversy surrounding the Second Amendment.

2. Work with a partner to research each of the legal decisions below. Then prepare a short oral presentation on one of them.

   United States v. Miller (1932)
   Quilici v. Village of Morton Grove (1962)
   Lewis v. United States (1980)
   Gillespie v. City of Indianapolis (1999)
   United States v. Emerson (1999)

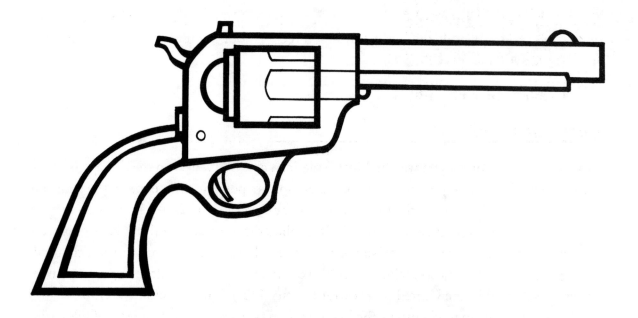

Who's Watching Your TV?

What's the Issue?

How much television do you watch? Most American children watch on the average of three to four hours daily. Most experts think that television is a powerful influence on the behavior of children. That theory was the motivation for the development of technology to restrict the kinds of television that children watch. It is called the V-chip, or anti-violence chip. It is a piece of hardware placed in television sets that can detect encoded information that will block programs with objectionable material like violence, sex, or adult language. All new television sets sold in the United States after January 1, 2000, must contain V-chips.

According to its manufacturers, the V-chip doesn't solve all of the problems of television viewing. Parents and caregivers must work to use the technology properly. Using the TV rating system that is now in place, parents can determine which programs are appropriate for children of various ages, but they must program the V-chip to "screen out" programs whose ratings they feel are unsuitable for their children

The main issues in the V-chip debate concern parental responsibility, whether the government should interfere in people's lives, and whether or not the V-chip is a form of censorship.

Supporters of the V-chip point out that children are exposed to about 8,000 murders and 100,000 acts of violence by the time they complete elementary school. Although television violence is not the only cause of aggressive or violent behavior, many studies on the effects of television on children and teenagers show that it is a significant factor. According to the American Medical Association, the National Institute of Mental Health, and the American Psychological Association, many children become immune to the horror of violence and gradually accept violence as a way to solve problems. Also, some children imitate the violence they observe on television, or develop excessive fear of violence.

Not all parents want to use the V-chip. Some feel it is a form of censorship for both the viewer and television producers. They feel that it is another form of interference into their lives. They suggest using other blocking devices, such as lock-boxes that deny children access to certain channels. However, supporters are quick to point out that the V-chip is simple to operate and that there is an on/off switch, so censorship is not an issue. Rather, they say, the V-chip allows parents to make better-informed decisions about what their children watch.

When the V-chip was first introduced, broadcasters were concerned that it would reduce the audience for their programming and thereby reduce their advertising revenue. They feared that the audiences for even adult-themed programs would shrink. They were concerned that the V-chip couldn't distinguish between programs that use violence for the sake of violence, and those that document historical violence, like the movie *Schindler's List*.

Ironically, people opposed to the V-chip feel that it makes it too easy for parents and caregivers to ignore inappropriate programming. They say that parents should always monitor the programs their children watch, because some inappropriate material will get through even with the V-chip in place. Some research supports the notion that adult supervision is the most effective antidote to the effects of TV violence. On many kibbutzim in Israel, all the children watch television together, and there is always an adult present to explain to them what they see. That's quite a contrast to what takes place in American homes, where kids settle down in front of the TV, alone or with their peers, unsupervised.

Most parents, educators, and doctors feel strongly that the amount of time children spend watching TV should be moderated, regardless of the content, because it decreases time spent on more beneficial activities such as reading, playing with friends, exercise, and hobbies.

1. Assess the popularity of various television programs aimed at students your age. Make a list of five or more shows. Next to the title of each show, explain the main theme or setting of the show, why you think it is popular, and whether or not you think it is appropriate for children your age.

2. Conduct a survey of opinions of students, teachers, and parents on V-chip technology. Analyze the responses to the survey, and write a summary of the results. Below are some questions you might include:

   Do you think the V-chip is a form of censorship?

   Would you use the V-chip?

   Do you approve of the decision to have the V-chip installed in all television sets?

   Do parents understand how to use the V-chip?

   Is the V-chip effective?

3. If you were a parent, what rules or guidelines would you establish to determine what television shows your children would watch? Explain your rules and guidelines, and the reasons for them, in a short essay. Share your essay with the rest of the class.

4. Debate the proposition "Television for children should be regulated using the V-chip." (Use the "Tips for Discussions and Debates" on page 8.)

5. Create a flyer or magazine advertisement, or tape a public service announcement, about one of these topics:

   The V-chip and its amazing ability to filter out inappropriate television programs.

   The intrusive nature of the V-chip.

1. Study the TV ratings system below (TV Parental Guidelines). Then improve upon these guidelines by creating your own rating system. Your system should be fair and helpful to both parents and children, and should define several categories for rating television shows. Create a name or symbol for each category, and give an example of a television show that would belong in each category.

2. Different countries have different philosophies on whether or not television for children should be monitored. Conduct research to find out what rules and regulations other countries have on monitoring television. Compare and contrast your findings in the form of a chart.

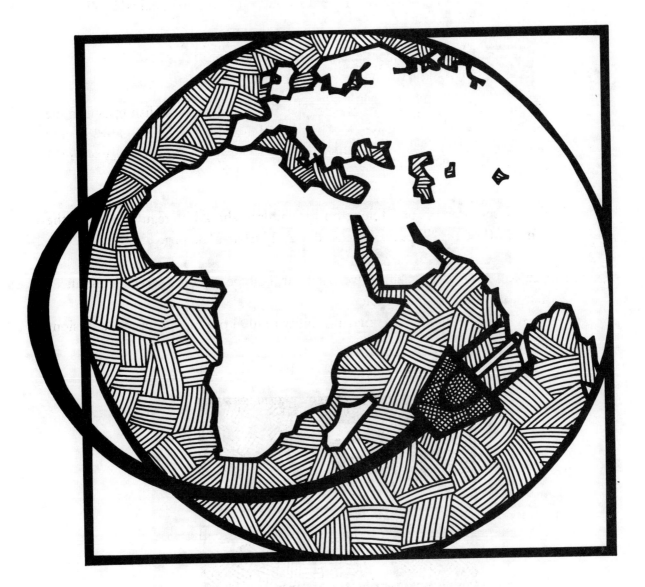

All Children (TV-Y)

The program is designed to be appropriate for all children, including children ages 2-6. Some shows with cartoon violence are rated TV-Y. There is no content rating to let you know whether a TV-Y show contains violence.

Directed to Older Children (TV-Y7)

The program is designed for children ages 7 and above. Themes and elements in the program may include mild fantasy or comedic violence, or may frighten children under the age of 7.

Directed to Older Children—Fantasy Violence (TV-Y7 FV)

Programs in which fantasy violence may be more intense or more combative than in other programs in the TV-Y7 category will be designated TV-Y7-FV. Fantasy violence may be part of a cartoon, a live-action show, or a program that combines both animation and live action.

106

General Audience (TV-G)

Most parents would find the program appropriate for all ages. It contains little or no violence, no strong language, and little or no sexual dialogue or situations.

Parental Guidance Suggested (TV-PG)

The program contains material that parents may find unsuitable for younger children. Many parents may want to be present when their children view these programs.

Parents Strongly Cautioned (TV-14)

The program contains some material that parents would find unsuitable for children under 14 years of age. Parents are strongly urged to exercise care in monitoring this program and are cautioned against letting children under the age of 14 watch unattended.

Mature Audience Only (TV-MA)

The program is specifically designed to be viewed by adults and therefore may be unsuitable for children under 17.

Additional Propositions for Discussion and Debate

Government Topics

1. People should not be allowed to use cell phones while driving.

2. The Internet must be regulated to guard against duplicating copyrighted music, art, and prose.

3. The United States is obliged to take in the world's refugees.

4. Internet gambling should be outlawed.

5. Gaming casinos on American Indian reservations should be closed.

6. The use of marijuana should be legalized.

7. The age for obtaining a driver's license should be 21.

8. The federal government should subsidize art galleries, symphony orchestras, and dance companies.

9. Banks should offer credit to teenagers.

10. Flag burning should be against the law.

11. The Confederate flag is a symbol of racism and should be banned from flying over state capitol buildings.

12. Internet filters should be installed on public library computers.

13. The power of the presidency should be significantly curtailed.

14. The words "under God" should be removed from the Pledge of Allegiance.

108

1. Global warming threatens the environmental health of our world.

2. The United Nations should regulate use of the world's rain forests.

3. Terminally ill people should have the legal right to obtain a doctor's help in ending their lives.

4. Rodeos (or circuses) promote cruelty to animals and should be outlawed.

5. The United States should adopt an energy policy that substantially reduces the consumption of fossil fuels.

6. The United States should increase its nuclear power capacity to deal with today's energy crisis.

1. Physical education should not be required for public school students.

2. Students can prevent plagiarism by not copying from others and not letting others copy from them.

3. Random drug testing should be approved for all school campuses.

4. School vouchers should not be approved because they will undermine the public schools and allow taxpayers' money to go to religious schools.

5. Year-round school terms should be abandoned.

6. Physical education is a humiliating course that rewards only the most athletic and competetive students.

7. Music and art should be eliminated from the curriculum because more time should be spent on math and reading.

8. Fast-food restaurants should be allowed to sell their products on public school campuses.

Philosophical Topics:

1. Freedom is always somehow restricted.

2. Science is the only way to gain knowledge of the world.

3. Computer viruses are as alive as real viruses.

4. The world is inherently imperfect.

5. Democracy is the best form of government.

6. Certain moral standards are common to all humanity.

7. Individuals are morally obligated to risk their lives for their countries.

8. An oppressive government is better than no government at all.

9. There is never a good reason to lie.

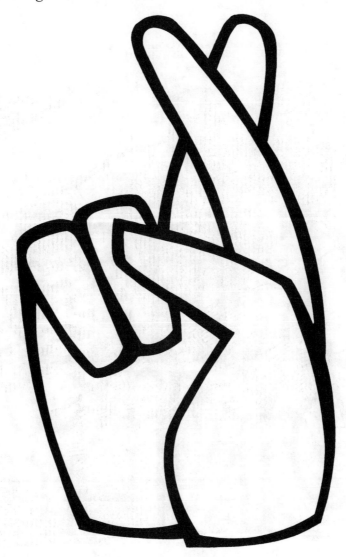

1. Women should not have the right to vote.

2. Each state may decide whether or not it will permit slavery.

3. Certain places, like restaurants, restrooms, and buses, should be racially segregated.

4. Creationism should be taught in science classes.

5. The Southern states should have the right to secede from the rest of the United States.

6. The United States should extend diplomatic recognition to the communist government of China.

7. Lands gained in war are the legitimate possession of the winner.

8. The United States government is justified in using force to remove Native Americans from the Illinois Territory.

9. President Andrew Johnson should have been impeached.

10. Columbus was an invader who exploited the New World.

11. The atomic bomb should never have been dropped on Japan during World War II.

12. The earth is flat.